A Quiet Country Town

A Quiet Country Town

A Celebration of 100 Years of Westland at Yeovil

To Phillip, we all did our bit and achieved a lot

David Gibbings

David Gibbings

Cover photograph: Doug Lloyd

First published 2015

The History Press
The Mill, Brimscombe Port
Stroud, Gloucestershire, GL5 2QG
www.thehistorypress.co.uk

British Library Cataloguing in Publication Data.
A catalogue record for this book is available from the British Library.

ISBN 978 0 7509 6242 1

Typesetting and origination by The History Press
Printed in Great Britain

A Dedication by:

The Rt Hon. the Lord Ashdown of Norton-sub-Hamdon GCMG KBE

'As well as being a world class aero-engineering and technology firm, Westland is the industrial heart of the community in Yeovil and South Somerset. I was privileged to work for a Westland firm in Yeovil and to represent the community in Parliament.

For anyone interested in the South Somerset area or in Britain's proud aero-industry, this comprehensive account is a "must read",'

Paddy Ashdown

Contents

Acknowledgements		9
Introduction		11
1. How It All Began	Derek James	13
2. The Westland Railway Siding	Derek Phillips	18
3. The RAeS at Yeovil	Dr G.S. Hislop	20
4. Saga of a Widgeon	Harald Penrose	23
5. What on Earth is a Wapiti?	David Gibbings	28
6. Wapiti Aircrew	James Kightly	30
7. Flight Over Everest	David Gibbings	33
8. Pterodactyl	Harald Penrose	36
9. Lysander	Harald Penrose	41
10. Spitfire and Whirlwind	Harald Penrose	46
11. W.E.W. Petter 1908–1968	Glyn Davies	50
12. The Bombing of Yeovil	Dilip Sarkar	54
13. The Good Neighbour	Graham Mottram	56
14. Normalair	Mike Bednall	60
15. Helicopters	O.L.L. Fitzwilliams	66
16. Here be Giant Killers	Jack Sweet	72
17. Wyvern	Harald Penrose	79
18. Rationalisation	David Gibbings	86
19. Westland 1947–1968	John Fay	89
20. Lynx – The Making of a Thoroughbred	David Gibbings	95
21. The Procurement Dilemma	David Gibbings	119
22. Exocet	Jim Schofield	123
23. Airborne Early Warning	Jim Schofield	128
24. Going for a Song	David Gibbings	138

25.	Ode to the Wessex	*David Baston*	142
26.	Putting the Record Straight	*David Gibbings*	147
27.	The Westland Affair	*David Gibbings*	154
28.	Working with the Italians/English	*Peter Dunford and*	
		Fiorenzo Mussi	159
29.	Airfield Noise!	*David Gibbings*	169
	Appendix 1: Aircraft List		174
	Appendix 2: Westland People		176
	Appendix 3: Pictures of Westland		182
	Bibliography	*Fred Ballam*	190

Acknowledgements

It is always pleasant, when one has been involved in a book, to discover that your efforts have not passed unnoticed, and that the author has acknowledged the contribution. For this book, which is an anthology, the authors are prominently named, and can be assured of my thanks for their fine work.

A number of my colleagues at AgustaWestland helped me on the way but I shall not follow the risky path of naming a few, in the knowledge that I would unintentionally miss someone out.

I will break that rule just a little: the basis for the cover was the work of Doug Lloyd; few books, publications, presentations or layouts are produced within Westland without his generous help. Simon Pryor controls the use of AW photographs, and the high standard of photographs available is due to him. Both these stars have my thanks as fellow artists, enthusiasts and valued friends..

It has been my privilege to assist Richard Folkes during the lead-up to the centenary. I have always admired positive thinking and good humour, and here I have met my match.

I am indebted to my colleagues from the Westland family past, and their brilliant young successors and of course that 'Parcel of Rogues ' who make up 'Flight Operations', pilots and engineers who knowingly or unwittingly have contributed to this book.

I would wish that those who started it all in 1915 could be aware of what they, we and the people of Yeovil have achieved, and long may it continue.

Introduction

So it is 100 years since the airfield was established and the manufacture of aircraft commenced at Yeovil. From that time onwards Yeovil ceased to be the quiet country town it had always been, and began to develop as an aviation centre.

As celebrating a significant anniversary would clearly call for a book, my own thoughts were that this should not be yet another catalogue of aircraft, but rather something that brought out the relationship between the aircraft company and the local community.

The formative years were devoted to fixed-wing aircraft; however, Westland has established itself as a helicopter company and now stands as a centre of rotorcraft activity within the UK.

The West Country has always been at the heart of the quest to fly. In 1848 Stringfellow flew his steam-driven model at Chard, and this event is generally accepted as the first flight by an aircraft operating under its own power. It is interesting to reflect upon the incredible rate of progress since that time. It took 50 years before the Wright Brothers were able to fly a mere 40 metres/120 feet.

However, thirty years later the DC-3 flew, capable of taking 30 passengers between cities, and little over thirty years after that Concorde was flying the Atlantic at supersonic speeds. By the mid-1980s, the Space Shuttle was taking man into space.

Although the development of the helicopter does not invoke the same excitement as the supersonic adventure, the creation of an aircraft that can take off and land on a given spot is a life saver in itself, and involves all the high technology available. It follows that the work going on within the factory compound and airfield at Yeovil today has advanced to a level comparable anywhere within the aerospace industry.

If one looks into the origins of any significant settlement at Yeovil, it becomes evident that it was beginning to expand with the arrival of the Romans and the traffic of goods along the Fosse Way, so there is cause for some amusement that maybe there has always been Italian interest in Yeovil from the very beginning.

It should be noted that for one third of the century we now celebrate we have been closely associated with the Italian company Agusta. It certainly should be noted that this is also reflected by the fact that Yeovil has chosen to twin with Cascina Costa.

A great deal has been written about Westland, and extracts from these sources have been selected for this book, and there are also several original items. Taken together they should tell a story, not only about the engineering, but about the people involved and the relationship with the town and local community.

When Westland decided to transform itself into a specialist helicopter company, the decision was influenced by the fact that here was a flying machine with only limited military potential, largely seen as lifesaver or means of transportation, a technology well suited for a 'Swords to Ploughshares' philosophy.

The armed helicopter that has evolved from such good intentions is now a force to be reckoned with, but even so, for any major disaster in the world there is generally a call for helicopters to carry and place help where it is needed.

Although we have not experienced warfare on the scale of World War Two during the last seventy years, Britain has been to war on several occasions in Suez, Malaysia, Aden, the Falklands, the Balkans, Iraq and Afghanistan, and helicopters have played a crucial part in the action. Oil exploration on the scale that we now know it is totally reliant upon the unique capability of the helicopter.

Search and Rescue and Air Ambulance are now well established.

And to serve the UK, all but a few came up from Somerset!

NB An observation I must make concerns the number of technical terms that proliferate throughout this book. They are, I fear, the language of our profession, and in my opinion unavoidable in a book of this nature.

1 How It All Began

Derek James

In his book Westland – A History *the author Derek James opened with the following: 'on the way in which the Petter family established engineering into a quiet country town, that in turn evolved into the Aerospace Centre it has now become.'*

The South side of Yeovil Borough in the early 1900s. From an original drawing by Stan Seagar, a designer who joined the company in 1917.

'What's in a name?' asked William Shakespeare in *Romeo and Juliet*; he then went on to opine that whatever name we give to a rose it still smells as sweet. Most aircraft manufacturing companies originally bore the names of their founders: Sopwith, A.V. Roe & Blackburn, Boeing, Northrop, Loughead & Potez, Fokker, Tupolev, Mikoyan & Gurevich. Others used the location of their factories: Gloucestershire Aircraft, Bristol Aeroplane, Sud Aviation, Reims Aviation, and Fabbrica Italiana Automobili Torino. Then there was – and still is – Westland, a name first used in 1915 by the wife of Percy Petter who, with his twin brother Ernest, was to establish an aircraft business that retains this name 100 years later – although it is now joined with Agusta, whose history stretches back to 1923.

The Westland story began way back in 1868 when a young Somerset man, James Bazeley Petter, was given a thriving Yeovil ironmongers business as a wedding present at his marriage to Charlotte Waddams. As the business, named Haman & Gillett, prospered, James and Charlotte produced fifteen children, of which the third and fourth were twin boys born on 26 May 1873. They were christened Percival Waddams and Ernest Willoughby. About two years later James Petter took in a partner, the business name was changed to Petter & Edgar and agricultural equipment was added to its activities. Petter also took over the Yeovil Foundry & Engineering Works, which among other things, produced castings for the Nautilus-patented fire grate, its success being assured after Queen Victoria had these grates installed in her homes at Osborne on the Isle of Wight and at Balmoral.

Some twenty-five years before James and Charlotte were married, Somerset was witness to a number of aeronautical events resulting from the experimental work of John Stringfellow and William Samuel Henson, a visionary of air travel and fellow experimenter with Stringfellow. Both lived in Chard and devoted much time to steam-powered models. It was in the year of James Petter's wedding that one of these was credited with being the first heavier-than-air model to fly (although doubts have been cast on this achievement more recently) and was shown at the Royal Aeronautical Society's first exhibition in London's Crystal Palace. The county was also the site for a number of nineteenth-century balloon flights and experiments with model gliders. Without doubt these and other aeronautical activities caught the attention – if only subliminally – of Percy and Ernest Petter.

While still a pupil at Yeovil Grammar School, Percy was developing his engineering skills by building rudimentary, hand-cranked 'vehicles'. On leaving school he worked in his father's Yeovil Foundry and became its manager when he was aged 20. Percy later admitted that he had lacked experience and depended heavily on the foreman, Benjamin Jacobs, a multi-talented craftsman who, in 1894, built a 3hp single-cylinder oil engine to power Percy's 'horseless carriage'. This was an old four-wheel horse-drawn phaeton, a light open carriage named after Phaeton of Greek mythology, who was the son of Helios the sun god and notorious for his bad driving of the sun-chariot! Completed the following year, this motorised phaeton went on show in the Crystal Palace and took part in the 1896 Lord Mayor's Show. The success of Percy's project resulted in his father launching the Yeovil Motor Car & Cycle Co. Ltd in a purpose-built factory at Reckleford. Ernest was given administrative responsibility for this new enterprise, plus the Yeovil Foundry and the 'Nautilus' fire grate businesses. Future prospects looked good and the twins' brother, Hugh, was charged with promoting sales. Percy Petter recorded the following encounter: 'I remember a day when Colonel Harbin of Newton House asked Hugh how the cars were getting on. "We're still pushing them," he replied. "You usually are when I see you out with one," said the Colonel!'

However, this venture into motorcars was a financial disaster. An analysis of the company's businesses revealed that engines were the most profitable products and a £7,000 bank loan financed production of 1hp and 2hp oil engines, initially aimed at dairy and agricultural applications. It was in 1898 that Percy Petter publicly revealed his interest in human flight when he presented a lecture on the subject to members of the local YMCA in Yeovil Town Hall using lantern slides and models.

A more worrying financial crisis arose in 1901 when Ernest Petter reported that all three businesses, particularly the engine side, had contributed to a £3,000 loss. This time, friends came to the rescue with loans totalling £4,000 and within the year the company, now renamed James B. Petter & Sons, had reversed its fortunes with a £2,000 profit.

Meanwhile, Percy and Benjamin Jacobs, now the chief engineer, often had ultimately fruitless discussions about designing an engine for an aeroplane. Percy also built a device consisting of a powered vertical revolving shaft with four horizontal arms carrying box kites to carry out experiments to attain vertical lift. These were short-lived due to the need for him to concentrate on the company's engine business. Nevertheless, they were harbingers of rotary-winged flight in Yeovil some fifty years later.

In 1910 Petters Ltd was registered as a public company to carry on the business of making oil engines. As the demand rose so did the need for larger production facilities. There was no more space at Reckleford and another site was sought. One day Percy Petter, along with Mr Hardiman the foundry manager, visited a possible site at West Hendford. 'We went along a narrow lane which terminated in high wooden doors,' recalled Percy. 'Beyond them we saw a fine piece of meadowland sloping up gradually from the Yeovil & Taunton branch railway. It seemed perfect.' The upshot was that seventy-five acres were purchased by a specially formed small private company. Another of the twins' brothers, John, who was an architect, produced plans for a housing scheme, adjoining the foundry and factory, for employees. One afternoon in 1913 Percy took his wife and two small daughters to this field for the first turf-cutting ceremony. Because the site was located to the west of Yeovil, Mrs Petter gave the name 'Westland' to this new development. The foundry and the first part of the machining and erecting shops were completed during early 1914. Today, 100 years later, that building is still in use.

Following the outbreak of the First World War on 4 August 1914, the export side of Petter's business almost disappeared. However, as all talk of 'exports' died, the words on everyone's lips were 'military markets'. Soon this new business became more rewarding. During the autumn of 1914 many people in Britain believed that the war would be over by Christmas, but their hopes were soon shattered. On 21 December a German aeroplane made the first air attack on Britain, dropping two bombs into the sea near Admiralty Pier, Dover. A second attack, on Christmas Eve, resulted in a bomb exploding near Dover Castle. It was not until 31 May 1915 that a German Zeppelin, LZ 38, made the first attack on London, killing seven civilians and injuring twice that number. But before then, during early April, Prime Minister David Lloyd George had revealed to a shocked House of Commons that there was a serious shortage of materials and equipment with which to continue fighting the war, and called for action to remedy this.

This news was received with some alarm in Yeovil and the Petter brothers made an immediate response. They proposed to their Board of Directors that their entire manufacturing facilities should be offered to the Government for the production of whatever was needed. There was only one dissenter so a letter was sent to the War Office – which ignored it – and another to the Admiralty, which immediately asked for a meeting with the Petter brothers. Within days the twins found themselves in London, talking with three Lords of the Admiralty and two high-ranking civil servants. Ernest recorded that the expressed need was for floatplanes, and that he and Percy were asked if they would produce them. Ernest wrote:

We explained that our experience and factory were not exactly in line with their requirements but that we were willing to attempt anything which would help the Country. 'Good,' said they. 'You're the fellows we want; we will send you the drawings and give you all the help we can. Get on with it.' So we got on with it.

The Admiralty instructed the company to send representatives to the Short Brothers' factory at Rochester to see the type of work to be undertaken at Yeovil. Almost certainly it was Oswald Short who explained the techniques involved in the construction of aeroplanes, particularly the Short 184 floatplane. Percy Petter later confessed that when he saw the nature of the work 'My heart nearly failed me', but his brother John and Mr Warren, a Petters foreman, had no doubts that they could organise production of such machines. However, an experienced aircraft engineer was required to head this new Petters venture and, after a diligent search, 46-year-old Robert Bruce joined the company to manage it. Bruce had been manager of the British & Colonial Aircraft Co. at Filton, Gloucestershire, but, as a Royal Navy Volunteer Reserve Lieutenant, he had become an Admiralty inspector with the Sopwith Aviation Co.

Bruce's immediate task was to build twelve Short 184 floatplanes powered by 225hp Sunbeam engines. It was to take all of his skills and experience to convert Petters' workforce to aircraft manufacturing. This was not so much a milestone in Petters' history as more of a signpost that was to point the path of the company's future in two directions. Petters' board decided that the new business would operate as a separate, but still wholly owned, unit with Bruce controlling the commercial, technical and production activities. As such, it needed a new name rather than to appear to be just another department of Petters. There is a rather romantic little episode which Sir Ernest Petter described in the company's house magazine in September 1936:

> Twenty-one years ago last April three men walked down to the corner of a field outside Yeovil where there was a small farm hut. One of the three – the author of this little story – opened the door of the hut and solemnly said, 'This is the Westland Aircraft Works.'

Undoubtedly he had remembered the name Percy's wife had first chosen for the proposed housing and works development. The foregoing story marked the parting of the ways for Petters' diesel engine business and its aircraft interests. The history of the former business is not for these pages; suffice it to say that, having weathered numerous associations, take-overs, the closure of certain Yeovil-based undertakings in 1939, several moves, amalgamations and near closure, diesel-engine manufacture was vested in the hands of Lister Petter Ltd in Dursley through a 1988 merger with this long-established Gloucestershire engineering company.

To meet the 1915 order for floatplanes Bruce needed a workforce. Some employees moved from the Nautilus factory and a number of woodworkers and engineers were recruited from local companies. One of the early pieces of equipment, which Robert Bruce had installed, was a 'wind channel', or wind tunnel, for the technical office. An important appointment was that of Arthur Davenport, a Petters engine designer who joined the new company in June as Chief Draughtsman. He was soon sent to the Royal Naval Air Station at Sheerness to measure and examine a Short 184 floatplane. In addition to Westland Aircraft Works, representatives of four other manufacturers who had been given contracts to build these aeroplanes were also there. They were Frederick Sage & Co. of Peterborough, Mann, Egerton & Co. of Norwich, Phoenix Dynamo of Bradford, and S.E. Saunders Ltd on the Isle of Wight. Their task was to make drawings of the structure and components so that their companies could build these floatplanes.

Production of Short 184 by Westland began early in July with the first aircraft being completed in time for delivery on 1 January 1916. It was dismantled and taken on horse-drawn carts to Yeovil Junction from where it went by rail to Hamble on the shores of Southampton Water for assembly and test-flying. It is believed that this particular aircraft was delivered to the Royal Naval Air Station on Calshot Spit. The fourth Westland-built Short 184, and the only one of its type still surviving, has a special niche in the history of naval aviation. On the afternoon of 31 May 1916 this aircraft took off from the seaplane carrier HMS *Engadine* during the opening phase of the Battle of Jutland. Despite very limited visibility the pilot, Lt F.J. Rutland, and his observer Assistant Paymaster C.S. Trewin, identified three enemy cruisers and ten destroyers whose position and course were reported to the British fleet. This reconnaissance flight proved a major milestone in naval air warfare. The pilot, who was subsequently awarded the Distinguished Service Order, became quite a celebrity in the Royal Navy and was dubbed 'Rutland of Jutland'. He was commissioned in the Royal Air Force after its formation on 1 April 1918 and became an authority on aircraft carrier operations. However, MI5 records recently made public have revealed that, from around 1934 until the beginning of the Second World War when he was living in the United States, Rutland spied on the US Navy for the Japanese. He returned to Britain and was interned until around 1944 when he was released.

Before the twelve Short 184s had been completed, Westland was given an order for twenty Short 166 floatplanes which were similar to the Type 184 but of an earlier design. Unfortunately Shorts was not able to provide a full set of drawings for the Type 166 and Arthur Davenport wasn't given the opportunity to measure a Short-built example. In addition, the twenty Westland 166s were to be built without the under-fuselage torpedo-carrying gear, which meant that Bruce and Davenport had to undertake some redesign work.

Westland had become an aircraft company.

2 The Westland Railway Siding

Derek Phillips

*'The movement of materials, spares and often, complete aircraft was necessary once aircraft man-
ufacture began on the Yeovil site. In 1915 the movement of such goods was very different to the
network of road transport and courier services now available.*

*From the outset Westland maintained its own railway siding, which remained in operation
until 1967, when the Yeovil to Taunton line closed.'* – Working Yeovil to Taunton Steam *by
kind permission from the author, Derek Phillips.*

Original drawing by Stan Seagar, Westland designer 1922.

A private siding agreement dated 29 March 1913 was made between the Great
Western Railway (GWR) and the well-known Yeovil firm of Petters Ltd, makers
of stationary, portable and traction petroleum engines, combined pumping engines,
electric lighting and power transmission plants. By 1912, Petters were running out of
room at their Nautilus works in Reckleford, Yeovil, and so they purchased some land
on the western side of Yeovil, near the GWR Yeovil to Taunton branch at Hendford,
on which they built a new factory. This was named 'Westland'. The firm began to
trade as Westland Aircraft Works, Westland Foundry, and the 'Petters' name was
reserved for their famous engines. During the First World War munitions were made
at the factory, and the first aircraft – seaplanes designed by Shorts – left by rail, as the
airfield wasn't ready until sometime in 1917. In the 1920s the Petters oil-engine business was moved to Westland from the Nautilus works.

The first locomotive purchased by Petters was a Manning Wardle 0-4-0 saddle tank, named 'EVA' and dating from 1866, which arrived sometime in 1920. Petters followed the GWR tradition and painted the engine green with yellow lining and a brass chimney cap. A Fowler diesel mechanical 0-4-0, works number 19425, was purchased in 1931, and fitted with a Petters 'ACE' three-cylinder engine. The locomotive was subsequently named 'ACE'. The Manning Wardle tank, 'EVA', was kept until 1935 and then sold for scrap. In 1935 Westland Aircraft Ltd was formed to take over the aircraft production from Petters, and more changes took place in 1938 when John Brown and Co. Ltd gained control of Westland Aircraft Ltd and Petters. Shortly after the takeover Petters was sold to Brush Electrical Industries Ltd, and the oil-engine division went to the Brush factory at Loughborough in 1939. The Fowler diesel, 'ACE', was transferred to the Brush sidings at Loughborough and stayed there until 1962. To replace her, Westland Aircraft Ltd purchased a four-wheel Howard locomotive to shunt the sidings. This locomotive was purchased second hand, and after a history of breakdowns, its engine was replaced by one from a Fordson tractor. Various engines were loaned to Westland by the GWR during periods when the Howard was out of service in the Second World War, when production was at its peak. These included, in 1940, an 0-6-0 saddle tank, No. 2195, built by Avonside in 1905, and in 1945 a Terrier AIX 0-6-0 Tank, No. 5 'Portishead', was on hire from the GWR from 14 to 19 July.

This locomotive, built by the London, Brighton and South Coast Railway (LB & SCR) in 1877, and originally named 'Gypsy Hill', had been sold to the Weston, Clevedon and Portishead Light Railway (WC & PLR) in 1926, was renamed 'Portishead' and became 'No. 3'. After closure of the WC & PLR:, it was sold to the GWR in 1940, kept its nameplate, but was renumbered 'No. 5'. The engine was based at Taunton, and later at Newton Abbot, before going into store at Swindon and then finally being scrapped.

When the branch was lifted from Curry Rivel Junction to Hendford in 1965, the line was cut just past Westland's siding gate, leaving the remaining stub to Pen Mill for freight traffic to Hendford goods and Westland's siding. The Howard locomotive lasted until the end of the railway services to the siding in 1967, and was then scrapped.

3 The RAeS at Yeovil

Dr G.S. Hislop

There has been a branch of the Royal Aeronautical Society, centred around Westland at Yeovil, since 1926. The branch represents a focal point for qualification and technical standards throughout the profession; many of the branch members have received some of the society's prestigious awards and medals.

The branch celebrated its 70th anniversary in 1986 with a gala dinner, and the branch president, Dr G.S. Hislop, who on this occasion was also in fact president of the main society, delivered an after-dinner speech that described the way in which the branch has developed in Yeovil.

The Royal Aeronautical Society, the oldest aeronautical organisation in the world, was founded 120 years ago, in 1866, in London. Sixty years later in 1926, when the total membership was 1,049, Coventry and Yeovil were the first two branches to be formed. There are now 13,000 members worldwide. Yeovil, which started with 113 members, continues to be one of the most active of the 30 branches functioning in the United Kingdom. Membership of the Yeovil branch continues to increase and is now at over 700, its highest level ever. The membership of the main society within the Branch has more than doubled in the last 10 years and now stands at 70 per cent of the total.

It happens that 1986 is also the 70th anniversary of entry into squadron service of Yeovil-built aircraft, the 50th anniversary of the first flight (12 June 1936) of the Lysander and also the 40th anniversary of Normalair Garrett. In his after-dinner speech, at the Golden Jubilee, ten years ago Mr O. Fitzwilliams said: 'I have to start by clearing up a discrepancy which is probably greater than is generally realised

– because this Jubilee celebrates the Anniversary of a meeting which was held on the 18th October 1926 and the body which was founded at that meeting was the Westland Aircraft Society:'

It is true that less than two months later the Westland Aircraft Society became the Yeovil Branch but throughout its life it was very much a company affair and, to begin with, one of its main and very successful objects was to hold lectures for Ground Engineers to meet the examination syllabus which had been published by the Air Ministry shortly before.

It was a very vigorous Society, and it held at least twenty-six and sometimes as many as thirty meetings in each six-month season up to at least 1933, but from the beginning it also contained a faction whose chief interest was to bring it under the wing of the Royal Aeronautical Society, and to the best of my knowledge we represent the only case of an already existing body which continued its own separate existence after being accepted as a Branch. To be specific, at a meeting held on 14 December 1926 the Council 'agreed to accede to the request of the Westland Aircraft Society to become the Yeovil Branch of the Royal Aeronautical Society' and on that day we became the 2nd Branch, following the formation of the Coventry Branch (who were mainly Armstrong Whitworth people) at about the beginning of March in the same year.

Under that arrangement the Yeovil Branch was entitled to retain its original identity and it did so up to the last war, with Rules and Procedures quite at variance with the normal practice of Branches. For example, throughout that period all correspondence from this end was on notepaper with Westland Aircraft Society across the top in large letters and Yeovil Branch, etc. in small print underneath and its Rules openly stated that Executive Directors of the Company were ex-officio members of the Committee.

As you can imagine Col Pritchard, the Secretary of the Parent Body, was absolutely opposed to that situation but in spite of that our relations with him and with the Society were excellent and you may like to know that on 21 March 1934 (about 7½ years after our foundation) Pritchard wrote to Victor Gaunt, who had been our founding Hon. Secretary, saying 'I really must congratulate you all upon the excellent show you always put up in every way. The Yeovil Branch is the envy of all other Branches and the standard to which they aim.'

The Westland Aircraft Society benefited greatly from its status as the Yeovil Branch, particularly from the fact that a large number of its lectures were published in the Journal. For example I found fifteen solid pages of Yeovil lectures in the Journal for January 1928. They were very good lectures and the lecturers who came here were amongst the most prominent figures in British Aviation at that time. Men like Rubbra, Fedden and Dowty were typical of that standard. The Yeovil Branch was also very appreciative indeed of the great help and consideration it received from Col Pritchard.

After the war, all reference to the Westland Aircraft Society was dropped but in 1963 it was realised that some distinctly odd Rules and Practices were still being followed. That discovery came about at a Committee meeting when Raoul Hafner, who was chairman in that year, found that Philip Tweed (who was then our Treasurer) had received the Branches Subsidy Cheque, made out to the Yeovil Branch, and was about to pay it in to a Yeovil bank account labelled Westland Aircraft Society. Having a certain Teutonic logic, Hafner naturally lifted that stone to see what was wriggling about underneath it and because of what he saw all our Rules and Procedures were, in that year, completely revised and approved by the Society, so that we became a fully respectable Branch.

Arthur Davenport was very anxious that the membership be brought to appreciate the great debt which is owed, not only by the Branch and the Westland company, but also by the Town of Yeovil and the whole surrounding district, to the Petter family for the decision they took to remain in the aircraft business after the First World War.

The membership should also appreciate the debt, which is owed to Messrs Fearn, Mensforth, Davenport and Wheeldon at board level and at a working level to such people as Fitzwilliams and Widgery, who steered the company into helicopters and cabin atmosphere control after the First World War!

So it is that during this centenary year, we celebrate nearly ninety years as a branch of the Royal Aeronautical Society, which as a learned body strongly influences the professional standing of our engineering staff and the way in which we are qualified.

★★★

In 1988 the Society Of Licensed Aircraft Engineers and Technicians (SLEAT) was incorporated into the Royal Aeronautical Society. The effect of this event was to introduce a whole new skill base. Concurrent with this event was the formation of a branch at Sherborne, which drew much of its membership from ex-SLEAT members. The Sherborne branch remained in being until 1996.

The expansion of Yeovilton led to the formation of another branch drawing its membership from the Royal Navy. The Yeovilton branch has prospered and maintains strong links with the Yeovil branch.

The death of Harald Penrose in 1996 led to the introduction of the 'Penrose lecture', a fitting memorial to a famous test pilot and one of the branch founders. The lecture is delivered annually covering subjects devoted to flight testing, engineering development or flight operations.

Another famous branch member has been recognised by the establishment of the Reggie Brie award for the annual young members lecture competition, the prize being generously donated by Elisabeth Brie.

The branch continues to enjoy generous support from AgustaWestland.

4 Saga of a Widgeon

Harald Penrose

In 1927, Westland introduced a two-seat monoplane called the Widgeon; it was a very attractive little aircraft, albeit expensive. Harald Penrose found it particularly attractive and retained one for his personal use throughout his flying career. A keen observer of the life that surrounded him in the air, he recalls the joy he derived from his flights in it, in his book, No Echo in the Sky.

A light aeroplane called the Widgeon became my greatest tutor. Setting the trend for Westland design which was to culminate in the Lysander, the Widgeon was a high-wing monoplane with a span of 36 feet and a top speed of just over one hundred miles an hour. With this machine I skimmed the countryside finding more unhurried view than any other aeroplane could give. From 1928 we flew together, learning secret after secret of the countryside and sky. I was a youth when I took her for her maiden flight on that far day of her first gay summer when they wheeled her, new and glistening, from the workshop. I was twenty years older, still dreaming myself unchanged, when I started her on the last, which ended a few seconds later in the disaster of leaping flames.

No other aeroplane was ever so well-suited for aerial observation, for there was practically nothing to obstruct the downward field of vision. The 'parasol' wing was placed on struts high above the body so that the pilot, seated far aft, had superb views, not only below, but upward as well. Yet there was more in the arrangement than unimpeded view. An exceptional degree of stability at the stall enabled the Widgeon to be flown with confidence at speeds slow enough to match the flight of many birds.

I liked to let this little aeroplane whisper through the air with engine almost closed, my gaze ranging far across both sky and ground. If the wind blew strongly it was possible to remain almost stationary over places of interest; yet, when the voyage of discovery was over, only a touch on the throttle was needed to bring her racing home at 100mph.

What tremendous discoveries we made, what wonders we saw! So many of those important and ever remembered first occasions belonged to the Widgeon. Again and again I watched with enchantment England take form from the coloured map in my hand. The buff and green paper picture became soaring brown hills rising from vales patched with meadows and patterned with hedgerow trees. But the map could not show the immensity of space as we sailed far and wide through the skies of youth, nor could it hint at the miracle of seeing this island with a comprehension that a hundred years of travelling on foot could never give. With each successive flight the individual characteristics of every county became more recognisable, until they were patently related to the geological structure of the land.

I began to see the countryside not merely as a cameo of exquisite beauty, but as the expression of the gigantic forces of expansion and contraction unleashed on the world as it grew from elemental form. Its later history was there to read as well; old boundaries of the sea, newer incursions, dried river valleys; turf-disguised mounds and marks of early man; Norman roads and Saxon paths, castles of conquerors uncertain of their hold, side by side with gracious dwellings of a more peaceful age, and the staring council houses of today's planned state. I saw too the grimness of industrial centres set like scars on the fair face of England, their smoke and fog covering a third of the countryside upon which the sun once shone unveiled through uncontaminated air.

I learned also the trick of height which dwarfs a river to a brook, or a mountain to a molehill: I knew then why the gods were omnipotent. Yet I found that other days could turn the mountain into fearsome walls, low-capped with cloud, where the Widgeon flew ensnared and only faith could find the valley of escape. And in the evening mist the estuary, which from 5,000 feet could be covered by my hand, was from a few feet high, a widespread trap of ugly waves, waiting for me to lose the vague horizon and sink within its shroud.

There were days, too, when the Widgeon took me into the world of cloud. Patiently we climbed, penetrated the overcast and became engulfed in the dark swirling vapour, travelling in a blind eternity that masked all sense of equilibrium. Suddenly the mist would grow luminous, become white, and in another instant we would burst through the top of the cloud into a world of brilliant light. As the little aeroplane climbed higher the clouds stretched wider and wider below, like an endless snowfield glittering under the arch of heaven. There, it was always as though we hung motionless, transfixed by the incandescent disc of sun on which no eye dare rest, so blinding was its majesty. The troubled world of people receded beyond thought and I felt reborn in that sublimity of space, oblivious of the truth that winged man was no more than a moth fluttering round the beacon lights.

Sometimes there were flights in the dusk, with the lights of villages and towns springing one by one in company with the early stars, until it seemed the countryside was scattered with glittering jewels. Sometimes we flew by moonlight, the hills and valleys grown strange and mysterious in the blanched light, and the sea a dusky silver framing the dark loom of the shore.

On many an occasion the Widgeon had borne me along that same coastline by daylight, until I knew the south like the back of my hand, and the east and west passably well. Over every small harbour I had flown, circling while I watched the way of men with ships. In storm and calm, sun and driving rain, at ebb and flood, I had seen the endless changes of the ocean's face, until at last I felt I understood a little of its power and inappeasable emptiness. We watched, too, the passage of the seasons, slowly flooding the length of these isles with green growth to attain the high tide of summer, and then ebbing to the regeneration of winter days. Twenty times we saw those black months of waiting and brooding on buds anew, until the countryside became suffused with the soft glow of richer colour that presages spring. Then the chess-board of ploughed soil would change texture as the earth grew hidden by thrusting shoots of new grass and tender wheat. Trees would froth into lacy leaf, and in the course of a week or even a day, the land would be transformed into eager, green, proliferous life. From the Widgeon I would see white blossom sweep the hedgerows and the fields grow starred with flowers. Yet to fly a little north could mean passing back from the wave of spring to find the buds still waiting to unfold. But only for a little while; soon the whole land would be verdant and fulfilled and as spring drove ever northwards, summer followed close.

From the air we saw infinitely delicate transitions as summer grew mature. Tree and hedge grew darker, velvet meadows changed to tumbled swathes. Presently there was golden grain. How quickly the flush of spring was forgotten when squares of plough showed once more among the fields of stubble and sere green; and autumn made the landscape glow with bronze, painting the earth with strange dim magnificence, like the tarnished chattels of a once noble house. With the first touch of winter the coloured trappings disappeared, the last leaves fell and trees were transformed into black tracery. Yet as the aeroplane skimmed over the topmost branches I could see that the bare twigs held already in their swelling tip the promise of yet another reincarnation.

So the months and years came and went, with questing and fulfilment, sadness and happiness. All that time the Widgeon carried me on tranquil wings, revealing new beauty in every hour, trying to let me understand at least a little of the mystery, the cohesion, the marvel and the eternity of nature and the cycle of life. Often, of course, we forgot the passing of time and played, for we were light-hearted as the birds. The breeze whispered exciting wordless promises that set veins tingling. The controls were delicate as finger-tips which stroked and read the air. For a little while the Widgeon ceased to be a man-made machine, and I knew only that I had wings. Across the sun-filled sky we glided like skaters over ice, cutting voluptuous curves and airy figures, dropping a few feet above the aerodrome, sinuously twisting and sliding a handspan over the turf. Then up and up, breasting the air, towering like a peregrine after its stoop.

Ah yes! Many times we had seen the peregrine at play do that hurtling, in its pounce like a searing blue arrow, only to rocket upwards and away. At other times we found the bird soaring at ease, throwing circle after lazy circle on a thermal lift a mile above the world. Not only the peregrine but every bird of the skyways we watched as well. They were kinsmen but with an older prerogative than mine. Theirs was an understanding and an unthinking art, perfected by the evolution of a million years. Turning, crabbing, hanging at the stall, the Widgeon drifted far across the countryside whilst I studied the manner of a bird casually encountered. Or perhaps we might seek them in their haunts: herons on the network waterways of Sedgemoor; buzzards mewling above wooded Devon hills; this family and that of wildfowl sheltering in their hundred thousand on the winter floods; grey geese with singing wings. Sometimes we searched for strange birds such as harriers, knowing that success would be rare, but that the prize of discovery would be all the more valuable.

Always it was like that. Even the last flights we made together were in their way a triumph, for now it was high summer and we played with the birds as of old. It had been the Widgeon's unluckiest year. For months she had been laid up, initially to change her ancient engine for one of newer vintage, and then because she stumbled in her next flight, losing a wheel and breaking her mahogany propeller. When at last the Widgeon flew again, it was as though a pretty moth had emerged from the chrysalis of long hibernation, for she had been re-built and painted handsomely with silver and soft sky-blue.

Over a brilliant landscape, no whit less miraculous and beautiful than those of her twenty other summers, the Widgeon flew with the carefree wending of a butterfly attracted by the gold heart of every flower. I watched the world slide slowly past, bringing each minute a score of new delights. From the few hundred feet at which we flew, the countryside was intimate as a garden, yet with a broad and beckoning vista drawn clearly like a map. The old enchantment gripped me, and I counted myself lucky to be of a century which at last could look at the world from the skies and see secrets known to a hundred million years of birds, but never before revealed to man.

The air was buoyant as the sea, but smoother than the stillest pond. Expanded by the earth's heat it shimmered upwards, bearing on its steady up-currents many insects and birds. On restless wings swallows flashed steel-blue as they tilted in the sunlight. Above them the dark crescent forms of swifts carved across the sky as they hawked the gauzy *diptera*. But though in numbers far exceeding other birds, the swifts and swallows were not alone in exploiting the heated air. Kestrels hovered on the breeze, silhouetted fox-red against the green of turf and shrub, their wing-tips blue. Where the woods were wildest on the hillsides, buzzards lightly circled on upspread wings, lifting steadily until they were high specks. Away to the north, above the water meadows, a heron sailed, dark wing-pinions flexed to pointed tips which gave no beat in half a mile. With all these birds, as well as the circling rooks, the Widgeon played on each of these last few flights; but mostly she flew contented and alone, wrapped in her dreams, happy to press and lift against the warm, calm air of yet another summer.

No new discoveries, no first encounters, no sudden revelation, no high adventure: only those three flights of tranquillity over the fairest country of all the world. All too soon it was the end. For the last time those silver wings had borne me through the limpid air, and I came sliding down in sighing curves to land lightly upon the new mown turf. I switched off the engine. Silently she stood there, facing the little breeze, while I flew another, newer aeroplane, forty times as powerful and five times more swift. The Widgeon waited, perhaps in jealousy, fearing I had given my heart to a new love, not dreaming that none can compare with the old. And everywhere birds were singing and calling her, for had we not sought and followed them everywhere?

Presently I was ready to go home. I swung her propeller. The engine gave a sudden, all too vigorous roar. Before the man standing by her switches could cut the power she was moving and running away. I flung myself at the cockpit and clambered on to the steps. But the ecstasy of the summer was nerving her, and high above was the wild cry of the mewling buzzard. She flung me off, and pilotless skimmed the ground, for the last time pressing herself against the breeze as she lifted.

So little a freedom this, so short a flight, so quick the end to aspiration. Twenty yards, fifty, she flew by herself – rocking a little, turning uncertainly. Then she swung tighter, and, only a few feet off the ground, went crashing full-tilt into the side of a shed. The roar of her engine died. Silence a moment, broken only by the song of a thrush – and then, under a pall of black smoke a great yellow flame leaped up, higher and higher. Her silver wings vanished, her gay, blue body became a stark black skeleton. Within three minutes there was only smoking wreckage, a last flickering flame, and a burned-out hole in the shed.

A swallow flashed past, turning with airy grace from wing to wing. High and far away, I heard again the faint cry of the buzzard. From the copse at the end of the aerodrome drifted the muted talk of rooks. I looked high into the sky, and, saw the swifts still soaring on crescent wings.

The smoke faded and rose more slowly. But from the flames, from the ashes, no Phoenix arose – only ghosts of memories, and the haunting knowledge that there would still be other days and other flights, using this aeroplane and that, but none so loved as the little Widgeon who had taught me that flight was more than self-revelation, and greater than the materialisation of a happiness akin to ecstasy. She had let me hear the echo of the very universe. To fly was a form of worship, a discrimination of mighty patterns transcending human life, instilling in me the desire to share the vision which the Widgeon had first shown me when she and I were young.

I turned to her again. Above the burnt-out wreckage a last slowly rising column of thin smoke hung insubstantially against the depth of sky. When it had gone a longer chapter of my life was closed. I breathed farewell – to you, my Widgeon, and you and you and you bound inescapably with the pageant of her years, and yet I knew that this was not the end. The future breathed promise that there would be other days and other years, more and yet more, to gather to my heart.

5 What on Earth is a Wapiti?

David Gibbings

Aircraft naming has always been a serious business, a new aircraft frequently labours on with little more than its project number to identify it and it is not uncommon for a naming competition to be launched, this sometimes with amusing results: 'A Gannet is a sea bird that can fold its wings and dive into the sea.'

Then there is the dull practice favoured by many PR specialists giving the aircraft a number only, the idea is that this brings the company name to the fore, such as Boeing 747 or Airbus 380. 'The name "Wapiti" often brings about some amusement.' – A comment by David Gibbings.

In 1926, Westland responded to the Air Ministry requirement 26/27, for a two-seat general-purpose biplane with an aircraft based on the de Havilland DH9A airframe.

The DH9A had been in service since 1918, and Westland was the Design Authority for the type. The bid was successful and the new aircraft fulfilled its role, 'Policing the Empire' with distinction.

The name chosen for the machine was 'Wapiti'. The naming of British military aircraft followed rules laid down by the services:

Bombers and transports – inland towns.
Fighters – predator animals, insects and birds.
Flying boats and seaplanes – coastal towns.
Trainers – schools and colleges.

The rules were not enforced too rigidly, and there are many exceptions, such as Spitfire. Animal names generally were acceptable, and the general-purpose machines were given the names of less ferocious creatures.

Alliteration was a common practice favoured by companies. Westland were keen to have a name beginning with 'W'.

Thus it was that 'Wapiti' was chosen for the DH9A replacement. A Wapiti (*Cervus canadensis*), from the Cree language *waapiti*, was a large deer species native to western North America and eastern Asia.

It is a name that has always given rise to some amusement, not helped by the RAF airman's version 'What a Pity'.

Production of the 500 or so Wapitis kept Westland in business through the lean years of the 1930s depression.

At least you now know that it is named after a North American deer, and who knows? You may be glad of that information if ever you were on *Who Wants to be a Millionaire?*, *Mastermind* or are even in a pub quiz, and 'What a Pity' if you had not been told!

6 Wapiti Aircrew

James Kightly

It seems hard to believe that almost ninety years have elapsed since the Wapiti was in service in its role 'Policing the Empire', and one of the most active areas was the north-west frontier of India, including Afghanistan.

The Royal Air Force had only been formed ten years earlier and the concept of professional aircrew beyond pilot and navigator had not been fully thought out.

The Westland Wapiti combined army co-operation functions with those of a general-duties bomber. It became famous as the type used in the RAF's Imperial 'Air Policing' role, in which a small number of two-seat bombers would make punitive attacks on the villages of rebel tribesmen, avoiding the use of a much larger, slower and more expensive army force.

The crews knew the aircraft as a 'What a Pity', but usually just the 'Wop' – Wapiti is actually another name for the large North American deer. The aircraft was a large biplane of conventional layout. Its two-bay wings and 420hp Bristol Jupiter radial engine enabled it to lift nearly 600lb of bombs – the Wapiti sometimes needed these advantages just to get airborne in 'hot and high' conditions around the periphery of the British Empire.

The type was affectionately remembered among the aircrew who flew it. Air Chief Marshal Sir David Lee recalled, 'It was easy to fly and, provided that liberties were not taken with it, it would submit to a certain degree of careless handling with consider-able tolerance.'

While the pilots were dedicated aircrew, there were no dedicated air gunners – so ground crew regularly flew in this role. Each aircraft had an assigned fitter and rigger, while the armourers were pooled. Which of them flew depended on the pecking order, but it was most common for armourers to fly, then fitters, then riggers. Fitters were popular passengers over the North-West Frontier because of their engine expertise. Corporal Aero Fitter J.S. Millman remembered the Wapiti fondly, but also that the rear cockpit had only a single safety strap. Turbulence could be so bad he was often down on the floor.

No oxygen masks

The crew usually flew wearing pith-helmets with the front cut away to allow them to raise their goggles. They had oxygen, but no masks: the oxygen was breathed through a rubber tube clenched in the teeth, and there were frequent nosebleeds as the aircraft climbed to high altitude. There was a speaking-tube, but in practice the crew communicated by thumping Morse code to each other on the side of the fuselage – a practice called 'tonking'. There was a prone bomb-aiming position, with a Mk IIG bombsight (or camera) below the cockpits; but it was rarely used, the pilot usually aiming and releasing the bombs from his seat.

The RAF had to prove Air Policing a success, as a new role for the young air force. Although experienced crews could find and hit the right target – even 'specific houses of tribal leaders, leaving the rest of the village unharmed', that was exceptional. Overall, though, the operations were highly effective – and, in 'blood and treasure', very economical. The landscapes around these operations were truly awe-inspiring, and flying the then newest weapons of war over some of the oldest battlegrounds in history must have been an amazing experience.

The office ...

The pilot's cockpit was conventional but draughty. It had the usual selection of controls and the instruments unorganised on the panel. The gunner's cockpit would seem incredibly sparse and unsafe today, with a folding seat, 'firing steps' and only a 'monkey wire' to hold the airman in. There was a rudder bar and a removable control stick. The Scarff gun-ring was often gunless, but the gunner was responsible for retrieving any messages from the message hook, as well as operating the Morse wireless.

I was there ...

Sgt Cecil Beeton 84 Squadron
'I was soon taking part in squadron training which ... included: supply-dropping, message picking-up, formation flying, spot landings, drogue-towing, air firing (front

and rear), bombing, dive-bombing, night flying (landing with searchlights, oil flares and wingtip Holt flares) and photography.'

Sid Sills airman Wireless Operator

'I was sometimes called upon to fly on test in the Wapitis after they had been stripped and rebuilt, to check out the antediluvian radio, sometimes with an Indian pilot, an experience in itself … The aircraft's short landing, take-off ability and climb were phenomenal. I can assure you that pilots found it a mind-boggling experience when they converted to the Blenheim.'

Sgt Cecil Beeton 84 Squadron

'As John Wolstenholme told me, life in the observer's cockpit was, at times, hazardous. With only a wire cable attached to a ring bolt in the floor of the cockpit to hold him in, he could find himself out of the aircraft dangling in space if the pilot performed a bad loop or roll.'

Want to know more?

The sole preserved Wapiti is in the Indian Air Force museum at Palam, New Delhi, while the RAF Museum has a Wallace fuselage on display. *Aeroplane* published a Wapiti Database section in July 2007, and a four-part feature in July–October 1994. As well as many Internet references to Air Policing, there is remarkable amateur period film by Gp Capt. Robert Lister in a BBC interview: http://airminded.org/2010/04/20/wings-over-waziristan/

Nothing personal

Miranshah tribesmen who shot at the aircraft with home-made rifles of exquisite beauty would also come to the landing ground to sell food, firewood and souvenirs, being perfectly friendly.

Vital supplies

The 'Desert Equipment' wooden crate contained water tins, tools, rations, a spare wheel, screw-pickets, footpump, jack, petrol funnel with chamois-leather filter and personal equipment. The famous 'goolie chit' was just as important.

7 Flight Over Everest

David Gibbings

In 1933 Everest stood unclimbed and indeed would remain so for a further 20 years; several attempts had been made, with considerable loss of life.

The growth of aviation indicated that it should be possible to fly over the summit, and gather photographic data from which maps could be made to assist a successful attempt.

This was the background against which the Houston Mount Everest Expedition was formed under the leadership of Air-Commodore P.F.M. Fellowes, DSO, and financed by Lady Houston.

Two aircraft were selected for the task; both were derivatives of the Wapiti, modified for the purpose. Built, modified and tested at Yeovil, the flight over the summit was successfully accomplished to receive worldwide acclamation, to a level similar to that generated by the first expeditions into space, some thirty years later.

The flight over the summit is described here by David Gibbings.

It goes without saying that to attempt to fly over Everest was totally dependent upon weather for climber and aviator alike and in the 1930s there was little in the way of professional weather forecasting available. Several days were spent waiting for the cloud to clear the summit, this it did on 3 April albeit with wind strength as high as 88mph at 24,000ft, with even worse conditions across the summit.

There was a Moth aircraft used by the expedition for weather reconnaissance and this reported further deterioration as the day progressed. It was decided to make a serious attempt and the two aircraft took off from Lalbalu at first light.

The observer in the PV-3 was working hard to ensure cameras were working properly, and immediately after take off started to manually assist the drive by hand cranking in short bursts every 20 seconds, a process he maintained for the next hour.

As they climbed they were beset with constant annoyance due to connectors loosening under vibration, these were put right with what can only be described as 'bodging' with a screwdriver.

Camera equipment, heating, and oxygen, all required attention as the aircraft continued to climb at subzero temperatures with the aircraft struggling to maintain basic handling stability.

The oblique views from the side windows were tantalising, Blacker was keen to obtain some good shots with a small Kodak hand held cine camera, but the large vertically mounted cameras had priority.

Blacker's activity during the run towards the summit must have been frenetic and physically exhausting, obtaining oblique shots with the hand held cine and still cameras, between the 20-second intervals for the fixed vertical units. All done in conditions of extreme cold and rarified atmosphere, and with the added responsibility of ensuring that equipment, including their personal life support systems which were primitive by modern standards were running properly.

At 31,000ft they were probably at the practical limit for the two Everest aircraft, already operating fully loaded (5,600lb – PV-3 G-ACAZ & 5,100lb – PV-6 G-ACBR) bearing in mind that there had to be some margin for control in the turbulent conditions that prevailed over the summit.

Piloting an open cockpit aircraft in temperatures below -50°C flying at 100knots, must in itself have been a feat of endurance. Every effort was made to maintain a flight pattern from which a photographic mosaic could be assembled, but flight into or close to the potentially dangerous plume had to be avoided. In the course of the flight over the summit drops of several hundred feet were experienced.

The lead aircraft G-ACAZ was flown by; Sqdn Ldr The Marquis of Douglas & Clydesdale, accompanied by Col Stewart Blacker OBE.

Westland PV-6 G-ACBR was flown by; Flt Lt David McIntyre, accompanied by Mr R.S. Bonnett of the Gaumont British News Corporation.

Everest as the world's tallest mountain was always viewed as one of the ultimate climbing challenges, all the more exciting because of its difficulty and potential danger. In the years between the wars it was a major goal for the leading climbers, such as Mallory and Irving or Shipton. Many died in the attempt.

By 1930, aircraft capable of flying at 30,000ft were available, at last man could actually fly close to the summit and photography was available that could make it possible to map the area. In 1932, the British Flight to Mount Everest was formed, many prominent figures of the day were involved including the author John Buchan. The team was selected to be led by Air Commodore John Fellowes DSO.

It was clear that the expedition would be an expensive undertaking from the outset, the selection and modification of the aircraft was high, and the installation of state of the art photographic equipment modified to withstand the hostile environment would add to this.

It was feared that the necessary funding could not be raised, but a donation of £15,000 from Lady Lucy Houston made it possible to proceed (Lady Houston had already financed the successful 1931 Schneider Trophy team, with the result that Britain won the trophy outright.)

A number of aircraft were considered and the Westland Wapiti series were chosen as most suitable because of their deep fuselage centre sections, and confidence that the required performance could be achieved.

Two aircraft were available, The Westland PV-3, which had been designed as a torpedo bomber for the Royal Navy, but was essentially a Wapiti derivative, this was chosen as the lead aircraft.

The Westland PV-6 was selected as the supporting machine; this aircraft was the demonstrator prototype for the Westland Wallace and as such was a high performance Wapiti.

The two aircraft were sufficiently similar to accept the conversion and were available at low cost when compared to new airframes. Both aircraft had important tasks to perform and each could handle the role of lead aircraft should that become necessary.

There followed a programme to modify the two machines, confirm performance, install and test the photographic fit, including its environmental protection and assess the crew's life support and heating systems. The electrical installation to support all this was very advanced by contemporary standards.

Westland's Chief Test Pilot, Harald Penrose was able to call upon Flt Lt Cyril Uwens who had taken the world altitude record to 43,976ft, for advice.

The two aircraft were shipped to India, accompanied by most of the 20-man team.

Fellowes, McIntyre and Clydesdale flew out in a selection of private aircraft (Gypsy Moth, Puss Moth and Fox Moth), a considerable undertaking in its own right.

The team and equipment assembled in Karachi (then India) in early March 1933. It took 3–4 weeks to assemble the aircraft, flight test and familiarise with the equipment and position at Lalbalu the base for the Everest flight.

The flights over Everest took place on April 3rd 1933, the photographs obtained were excellent, and at last man was able to look down on the inaccessible, the expedition had shown the way in which maps could be prepared.

The whole exercise was greeted with the same wonder and awe as manned spaceflight (28 years later in 1961) and only 8 years after that a man set foot on the moon (1969).

In the mountaineering world, twenty years were to pass before a man stood on the summit of Everest on Coronation day in 1953.

Westland always took pride in their part in the Everest achievement and the certificate awarded to apprentices upon completion and qualification, carried the image of the PV-3 approaching the summit until well into the 1970s.

8 Pterodactyl

Harald Penrose

In his book No Echo in the Sky *Harald Penrose relates the story of the initial flight tests with the Tailless Pterodactyl V. During the first attempts to fly the aircraft a structural failure during taxying, due to an error in calculation, had resulted in serious damage.*

Following a full design review and structural testing, the aircraft was declared ready for another attempt.

Fitters, designers and inspectors waited with me as I checked the loading. A faint threat of tension and restraint made talk brittle. At last they gave me the signal. I fastened on the newly packed parachute, took my helmet and goggles, and climbed into the tight cockpit. The sea of faces·became forgotten as I strapped myself to the seat harness. Time and date were written on my kneepad. Instruments and controls were checked and set. We were ready.

The galvanic force of a quite different and expectant vitality began to flow, turning thought and reaction to knife-edge intensity. I nodded to the men to crank the engine. A moment later the aeroplane surged into life, which fused and blended with my own.

Chocks away, I taxied cautiously towards the leeward corner of the aerodrome, conscious of the tightrope-walking motion of the tandem wheels. Already the sense of the machine's inertia and the manner of its response to the throttle seemed characteristics with which I had long been familiar. Wing tips trailing backward, wing skids rumbling, propeller glittering in the sun, the flying wing moved over the aerodrome, drawing a tendril of exhaust across the grass.

I turned by the hedge; steadily opened the engine, and let the acceleration build up in a half-mile run along the turf. We paused, and then slowly returned.

In the background of my senses there was faint mockery at the bold front of the moment. Though I might open the throttle with deliberation, this cynical inner voice jeered that this was no more than a prelude, bereft of any intention of making a full flight.

I made two more taxying runs at increasing speed, feeling the trim and stability, and trying to gauge the balance and effectiveness of the controls. Groping in the unknown I could only surmise that nothing was obviously wrong. A still faster run was made, and this time the machine gathered flying speed and lifted into the air, allowing me a brief feel of the response of the controls before I throttled back and the machine sank to the ground. After another hop I was satisfied that all was well and taxied in for the cowling to be removed and a last check made of structure and controls.

Half an hour later I taxied out again. At last the moment had arrived: the inevitable outcome of a long sequence of actions. I was buoyed with pride at being entrusted with a machine that represented the pinnacle of a new achievement, and exaltation at the privilege of my own function in the exploration of new worlds. Yet as I looked up from a last scrutiny of the instruments and gazed across the space of turf stretching ahead, I was pricked with the uneasy recollection that in its first trials this fantastic aeroplane had crumpled up. Instantly I tried to smother doubt with belief in the work of the very people whose logic had been proved fallible. Ah! whispered the voice, but how trivial a mistake! How great the consequence, came the echo.

I, of whom the arguing voices were a part, felt nevertheless remote from the debate. My life's force was preparing for the uplifting prospect of the next moment's move-ment into flight. I opened the throttle. Power poured through the machine, mounting in the quivering structure, mounting in my heart. The flying wing began to move.

Hold the control column lightly and still. Steer straight. Let her feel her way into the air. She is swinging: check quickly with the rudder: more – a bit sluggish in respond-ing. Steering is difficult on this bumpy ground. A glance to left and right shows the wings equally level, their skids trailing through the grass tops. Keep straight, straight – full rudder; centre; keep her straight; ignore the curious lurching. The grating of the skids has vanished. From the corner of my eyes I see they have lifted. The sweeping wings are already leaning on the air and letting it carry their weight.

Through the gale of wind that batters at my goggles, I watch the boundary hedge drawing swiftly nearer. This is the datum line of my consciousness. The turf is blurred and racing. Suddenly it is too late to stop. I can feel the animation of the wings, and the sleepy strength of the controls – but she *must* take-off, or a few seconds more will find her crashing through the hedge, the labour of thousand upon thousand of hours broken in an instant to crumpled wreckage: her story finished before it has begun

With an action that I knew, for all my concern, must be inevitable, a last jolt bid farewell from the ground and the wings were lifting her free, the hedge dropping and vanishing.

An immature eagle is trying out her wings. I concentrate mind and muscle on keeping her steady, waiting with held breath whilst she climbs on a long, flat trajectory towards the safety of the higher skies.

So still were my wings in the calm air that they might have been a painted picture; yet for all I knew they could be balanced upon a knife edge, since stability depended on a twist, built into those back-tapered tips and replacing the leverage of the usual tail-plane. If the wings were too flexible and altered their incidence when a varying load was imposed, anything might happen.

Very cautiously I rock the lateral control, then hastily centralise. It feels queer, as though a massive pendulum swings from a frail lever; so what will it do when I try more vigorously or move the combined ailerons and elevators together in a compound change of flight path? Presently is soon enough for the answer, presently, when there is ample height to give time for a parachute descent; meanwhile, keep her level and straight.

I took a breath. The noise of the engine thundered into my consciousness, silencing all thought for a few moments before it dwindled once more to an insulating drone that shielded me from sense and reality. With the untried fearlessness of all new and inexperienced things the aeroplane climbed onwards, as though it had for a long time been familiar with the engulfment of air that streamed and eddied over the taut fabric of the silver wings. My senses tuned to high pitch. I watched for the slightest movement, wondering with queer dispassion how the machine would react to the control forces that I must soon impose. With tolerant curiosity I looked towards the things that unhurrying time would bring for good or ill.

The green drift of fields and trees beneath the diminutive lower wing gave place to downlands unfolding and expanding as the aeroplane climbed still higher. There was no recollection that I had driven across them earlier in the day. In this springtime hour the land rested as though enchanted, serene with knowledge of the past and waiting with long patience for the years to come.

The altimeter moved its slow hand towards the 4,000 feet calibration at which the controls would be cautiously moved to gain level flight, and the critical moments would begin.

Without further thought we were there, and the aeroplane was level. Speed increased steadily whilst I progressively sensed its safety through the nerves of the flying controls. I removed my hand from the column. The flying wing flew level unfalteringly for many seconds. There was nothing immediately dangerous, and stability was good enough for further tests. I eased a little in my straps and breathed more freely.

I throttled back and slowed down; then scaled upward through the range of speeds again, this time rocking her laterally so that the wings drew tilted lines across the horizon at steeper and steeper inclination. The reaction was a little cumbersome, as though she was big and heavy in this plane, compared with the quick responses when I rocked her fore and aft. It was good enough to warrant further exploration.

I studied every visible section of the structure. All was well.

Once more I slowed the aeroplane, only to open the engine again and try the rudder through the range of speeds. She answered a little drunkenly, rolling as she did so. Something not right here. Leave it to check another day.

One further, vital step into the unknown remained. Before a landing could be made with the precision of confident knowledge, I had to know what would happen when the airflow over the wings began to break down at the machine's slowest flying speed. It was here that measurements on models tested in the wind tunnel had indicated possible danger. Slats like movable pinion feathers had been fitted at the edge of each wing tip to retain the lift and keep each side in balance. As the sweep-back of the wings placed the slats towards the rear of the machine, the leverage of the displaced lift was expected to tilt the flying wing downwards. The model tests, however, had shown that because of its forward position the centre section might retain excess lift and overcome this stabilising force. In this case the aeroplane would tilt uncontrollably upward to the stall, and fall into an irrecoverable spin. My mind concentrated into cold calculation and I began to close the throttle. The silent seconds dragged into an empty pause.

I raised the controller flaps higher and higher but there was little marked change in the incidence of the wing. Only the descending needle of the airspeed indicator showed that the attitude was altering steeply in relation to the invisible path of air. The balance of the machine grew precarious. The controls were ominously devoid of feel. Speed wavered at 45mph. I waited: waited for danger to leap, for violence, for the uncontrollable unexpected.

The control column jerked backward in my hand: the wingtip controllers flicked fully up, overbalancing and locking in position.

Now what? Spin? Stability intolerable? Controls impossible to return to normal? Wait … the A.S.I. stayed steady at 45. The altimeter was unwinding like a clock. I took a deep breath of relief. The machine was fully stalled, dropping with the measured safety of a parachute.

I pushed lightly on the column. A little stickily the big controllers moved down, and down, too, went the nose. I opened up the engine and, descending under easy control, the flying wing swiftly gathered speed. There was new safety in my wings, and the countryside smiled up, beckoning me home.

Enough for a first flight. Land now, and have the aeroplane examined before doing any more. Sufficient for the moment that she flew controllably and more or less conventionally. Next time she must be dived, but not today; not today for any of the unsuspected perils that I later discovered in the flexible ends of the tapered wings, which faster speeds were to twist upwards so that the downward extent of the controls was neutralised.

Back to the aerodrome I headed the machine. The triangular green space of the landing ground made it easy to find among the hedgerow-bordered rectangles of many small fields. With sweeping curves from left to right, the aeroplane dropped towards it, the canted tailless wings glinting with sunlight against the background sky. Many a man must be staring up amazed at this bat-like creature sliding through the heavens. Yet only when I turned in my seat and looked straight down the empty abyss behind, was it possible to realise that my aeroplane was in any way abnormal. I was conditioned to the strangeness.

Like a familiar, the Pterodactyl responded to my slightest wish transmitted by the lightest touch of foot and hand. Boldly it swept round the aerodrome, where, in the shadow of the hangars, stood the little group I had left twenty minutes earlier. To show that all was well I dived towards them, sweeping past close enough to recognise a few faces, then up in a wide climbing turn, gauging the one right moment which on closing the throttle would bring the trajectory of my glide within just sufficient clearance of the hedge to let the aeroplane settle on the grass close to those men who had dreamed of her, and built her, and at last had watched her fly.

Through the quiet evening I drove slowly home. It was good to linger. This was my country, my heritage of beauty, my own good earth. Here was the sentient world where my life was rooted. This was the world that held me in willing bondage, and this moment of renewal made me still more its own. Yet it was not reaction from any sense of strain that bonded me thus closer. The quiet curiosity and conjecture of what may happen in the unknown of any flying venture has no apprehension. Instead, one's insignificance in the vast amphitheatre of sky seems to draw a power beyond mortality, which restores the vision of the earth to greater brilliance.

9 Lysander

Harald Penrose

Of all the fixed-wing aircraft produced by Westland, the Lysander is probably the machine most symbolic of that phase of the company's product. Designed as a replacement for the Wapiti/ Wallace series of general-purpose aircraft that had been engaged in 'Policing the Empire', it was ill prepared for 'Blitzkrieg' and suffered badly when used in the front line at the outset of the Second World War.

After the fall of France, it was relegated to support duties, but its unique short take-off and landing capabilities made it ideal for special operations, transporting agents into occupied Europe. The scale and courage involved in this work has given the Lysander a special significance.

Harald Penrose relates his contact with the Lysander.

It was a night of stars and moonlight. Beneath my aeroplane the silvered land pricked with the scattered lights of villages and towns, made navigation easy. The air was so smooth that the aeroplane flew itself. A great stillness haunted the heavens.

Presently my home aerodrome drew close, a large, dark patch encircled on three sides by the lights of the town. A burst of three green stars soared towards me, and I fired an answering red Very cartridge. Aircraft manufacturers did not yet use radio.

For occasional night flying their pilots relied on dead reckoning and a flare path. But tonight for me there were no flares. I wanted to demonstrate that our new high-wing monoplane, the Lysander, could take care of itself.

I brought her round for the landing. The unique cantilever undercarriage was fixed, and the slats and flaps, which automatically extended at slow speed, also needed no thought. With a rumble of engine I placed her at 500 feet above the shadow of the aerodrome boundary. Speed was reduced and engine power increased to predetermined figures for a feather-like descent. More tailplane angle was wound on until the Lysander was trimmed in such perfect poise that I could take my hands off the stick and let her make the glide and landing unaided.

Down she sank, hanging on the air rushing through the wing slots. In spite of the moon, visibility was too indistinct to gauge height accurately. Our stalled, blind descent felt far too fast and my confidence in the drawing-board figures and calculations waned rapidly as I waited, my hand poised to grab the stick, and hoped the undercarriage would withstand the impact with the ground.

But the calculations were correct. As the tailwheel touched with a bump, I cut the engine, and the Lysander settled automatically on her main wheels. I let her run on until she stopped by the bright open doorway of the hangar. None of us dreamed as we pushed her inside that within a few years the Lysander's destiny was to be hundreds of night landings in enemy-occupied territory, with no more ground aid than three faint hand torches.

I flew the first of the Lysanders in 1936 when we were still building the delightful little Hector biplanes, with Napier engines, as the standard Army Co-operation machine. The Hector, however, was an adaptation of the earlier Hawker Audax fighter, whereas the Lysander had been specially designed to meet military gun-spotting requirements.

Within eight years to the final spy-dropping version in 1944, the Lizzie was to grow more powerful and some two thousand pounds heavier; but she remained always the same queer, amazing machine – noisy, smelly, heavy on controls, but able to crump and bump in and out of an absurdly small space whatever the load.

The advent of the Lysander marked a new epoch at the Westland factory. Robert Bruce had retired and his assistant, W. E. W. Petter, a young Cambridge graduate who was later to achieve much renown, took over the reins. Everyone was anxious that his first design should be a success. He tackled it with brilliance. Unconventional in detail, the new aeroplane followed the logical sequence of Westland monoplanes that had been initiated by Arthur Davenport in the original 'parasol' Widgeon, followed by the Wizard, Witch, Wessex, and the P.V.7 that had caused my parachute jump.

Designed, built and flown within the record space of a year from the acceptance of the tender, the Lysander made immediate history. Ultra-modern it seemed – yet within a few years most pilots regarded it with tolerant affection as a peculiar old hack, long antiquated. That is the fate of most man-made things. The machine of today's specialist becomes the toy of tomorrow's youngster – soon to be discarded for something better.

I liked the Lizzie. Her methods were unorthodox, and though they resulted in no great speed or climb, her slow-flying characteristic was remarkable. No other aeroplane of similar power and wing loading could operate from an area the size of a football pitch; but the Lysander's powerful slots and flaps made almost every small field a possible landing ground for emergency use. In a day when retractable undercarriages offering the refuge of belly landings were yet to be, the Lizzie's capacity for a parachute-like descent gave flying a feeling of incredible safety. Because of this, pilots would fly her in weather considered impossible for any other type in those days of limited ground control.

The convulsive rumble of the engine, the seeping of exhaust smoke from the depths of the cockpit, the rattle of windows and drumming of fabric sides, the ineffective jabbing of root slats at the propeller draught – these made up the familiar prelude to several thousand fascinating flights.

Take-off was simple. The only essential cockpit drill was to wind the large trimming wheel forward to the red mark on the scale. Failure could be fatal, for the tailplane had to be set to an extreme negative angle when making even a normal landing. If the tailplane was left in that position for take-off, the Lysander was apt to rear uncontrollably upwards, and several machines were wrecked as a result. This defect could not be readily overcome, and undelayed production was judged more important than the degree of risk to the pilot. Expediency has rationally governed such decisions countless times in the course of evolution of the world's aircraft. It is no good continuing development towards perfection for so long that the machine becomes obsolete before it is put into service.

Perhaps in these days the tailplane would have been ingeniously interconnected with the flaps, or made to vary automatically with air pressure – but at that time it was simpler to insist that the tail trim was a vital check.

There was little else to worry about. The top knob of three on the dash was pushed in to obtain fine take-off setting for the two-pitch propeller. A stiff crank opened the cowling grilles.

As the Lysander rolled forward over the grass, the inboard and wingtip slats opened wide, automatically pulling down the flaps. The machine climbed noisily in a tail-down attitude at anything between 60 and 80mph, and there was always a strong temptation at first to hold the nose down to gain speed. To do so, however, meant that the slats and flap closed, reducing the lift and making the aeroplane feel as though it had lost all buoyancy.

A similar danger lurked on the landing approach. Speed had to be reduced boldly or a disconcerting longitudinal rocking could be accidentally started. As speed dropped, the slats and flaps opened, and a large backward movement of the centre of pressure on the wing sent down the nose, putting up the speed again and automatically closing the slats. To resume his glide, the pilot had to pull back on the elevator – only to repeat the sequence. The result was often a very untidy landing.

On a gusty day, too, the Lysander was liable to pitch convulsively as the slats snatched suddenly in and out. Coupled with the extreme heat of the cockpit and the exhaustion of moving heavy controls, this trait could be a little wearing.

The machine's qualities, however, more than made up for these foibles. Unlike most contemporary aircraft of that period the Lysander gave an unimpeded view in all directions. Perched high in the nose, with the engine at my feet, and a vast amount of window all around, I felt at first as though I was projected into space. England lay visible in more perfect detail than ever before, whilst I loitered with slats fully extended, exploiting the Lysander's slow flight.

Since those earlier days when the Widgeon revealed the intimacy of England, the country's features had become part of my deep consciousness. Only a glimpse through clouds was needed to recognise my position with fair certainty. The style of houses, their stone, or brick, or timbers, the size and shape of fields and woods, the flow of the land, the aspect of heights and mountains, all played their part in pinpointing my place in the familiar tapestry. Yet on no two days was the scene the same. The texture was constantly changed by the wayward moisture of the atmosphere, sometimes softening the landscape with mist; at others encrusting it with glowing light, or with a limpidity that painted the far hills with brilliant clarity.

But if the Lysander was good for lingering over peacetime scenes she was too slow for fighting and war, whose threatening undertones we already were hearing. Full out, at her rated altitude of 6,500 feet, the top speed was a bare 180mph indicated. When pushed into a dive she became increasingly nose-heavy after 220mph, and with subsequent increase of speed it soon became necessary to wind the trim wheel back for recovery. At 300mph, control forces were almost beyond one's strength. At that limiting speed, the propeller screamed away far above its normal maximum because it lacked a constant speed unit. The structure vibrated with strain and the wing fabric between each rib bulged upwards under the tremendous suction. In earlier tests, in fact, the fabric came off altogether.

Although I had made many dives up to 340mph with the prototype, even before an adjustable tail was fitted, the sister machine nearly came to grief when it was sent, after brief handling trials, to Martlesham Heath for official test. In a dive to 280mph, there was a sudden crack followed by a violent lurch. The Lysander plunged steeper. Squadron Leader Collins, the pilot, pulled back on the controls and the machine slowly responded. Glancing over his shoulders he saw tattered remnants of fabric beating in the wind, and gaping holes in the wing structure.

Cautiously, he slowed the machine. The slats jerked open, the flaps came down. Soggy and unresponsive, the Lysander turned into a hurtling glide and Collins managed to reach the aerodrome and land at very high speed. The top surface of the wing had been stripped almost completely bare of fabric. Only the pilot's skill, the slats and wide leading edge of the spar had brought him home. Collins was awarded the A.F.C.

Suddenly the days of dreaming above a quiet England were wiped out. The long, golden time had closed. We were caught in a new web of life and death, and nothing could be done about it. Testing became a relentless task, where weapons must be rendered perfect for brave men. No more leisure. No more sailing for its peace. No more flying for its beauty and adventure.

And yet, even now, there was still the mind's escape, the impact of vastness and solitude, the consciousness of a power beyond oneself, which sprang not from fear of death, but from love of life that in those high places was stripped of the wrappings which shield it from earthly awareness of eternity. To all who flew, flying was an intensification of life. That was the reward of the many, whose wings for the last time reached towards the stars and nevermore returned.

Through those years of war the Lysander flew on. Her anachronistic role of spotting for guns in the strategy of outmoded battles changed to that of a defensive fighter with cannon in its wheel spats ready to rake the English beaches if an invader came. Relegated to target towing, she was subsequently reprieved and found a valuable and merciful mission as an Air-Sea Rescue aircraft. Her slow-flying ability enabled dinghies and supplies to be dropped accurately, whilst fast motor launches were directed to the rescue.

Presently her characteristics of slow flying, short landing run, and quick take-off, came into their own. On moonlit and starry nights the black-painted Lysanders, fitted with a long-range tank beneath the undercarriage legs, made many a gallant flight from Bedfordshire into enemy-occupied countries. More than 300 agents were flown to France alone, and 500 brought back to England. Like moths, the Lizzies travelled through the dim night by dead reckoning, to find somewhere in the dark landscape three electric battery torches set in the form of a letter L, 150 yards long, by 50 yards broad.

A prearranged Morse signal blinked. Slowly the Lysander groped down into whatever ground lay beyond the foot of the dim lights. In less than three minutes the machine would be off again and the field shrouded once more in darkness that hid a group of Frenchmen in the resistance movement welcoming a newly dropped agent.

The last I saw of the Lysander was on a winter's evening in the final year of the war. In the darkened control tower we awaited the return of one of my friends in the spy-dropping squadron. We were a little anxious. For three hours the Lizzie had been humming through stormy darkness. Because the weather was so bad, it had been the only aircraft to fly from Great Britain that night.

Presently we heard the familiar note of its engine. Like a dynamic shadow it made a circuit under the low, dense cloud that hid the moon. No word passed because the single VHF radio had failed. Recognition lights flickered and the Lysander emerged from the darkness on the broad band of the runway floodlight, which had been quickly switched on.

I watched the silhouettes of two vague, shadowy figures climb stiffly from the rear cockpit and hurry into a car. At once it began to move and the noise of the engine speeding towards London faded into the silence of the night.

10 Spitfire and Whirlwind

Harald Penrose

In 1940 the German raid on Southampton destroyed the Spitfire factory; a potential disaster was only averted by swift action by the Ministry of Aircraft Production, who set up a number of shadow factories, one of which was Yeovil, where limited Spitfire production was already in hand. Throughout the Battle of Britain, Yeovil became a centre for Spitfire overhaul and repair.

In his book No Echo in the Sky, *Harald Penrose relates his first encounter with the Spitfire. Yeovil was subsequently one of the main centres for the design, production and modification of the Seafire, and over 2,500 Spitfire/Seafires were built here.*

In soft sunshine I walked across the heather clumps fringing the tarmac apron at the Aircraft and Armament Experimental Establishment at Martlesham to gain experience of the latest conception in fighters.

This was the shape of things to come, the low wing cantilever monoplane, made possible by retractable undercarriages and new alloys for the fashioning of smooth-skinned structures combining lightness and strength.

For long years scientists and engineers had dreamed of this approach to the ideal bird form; and now, in the year 1938, the urgency of the international situation was removing the last prejudice in favour of the traditional biplane, and speeding the evolution of the most famous fighter of the Second World War.

The temporary, fixed-pitch, wooden propeller did nothing to mar the ultra-modern appearance of the lineal descendant of the S6B, Schneider trophy winner. Smooth as ice and glistening in blue-grey paint, the lines of the Spitfire looked exactly right, a testimony to the awe-inspiring repute of its speed.

The interest and the hidden questioning at flying an unknown machine steeled into the fatalistic confidence all pilots recognise, as I clambered on to the wing and squeezed gingerly down between the semi-circular windscreen and the pushed-back hood. Settling into the tight-fitting metal shell, I let the hard newness of its touch filter through my consciousness. There was strangeness in the upright sitting posture, in the queer smell of different paint and the sharp tang of hydraulic fluid. My glance outside took in the relationship of wing and ground. The view ahead was blocked by the broad, flat nose.

Everything felt disturbingly unfamiliar, but the sooner I made a start, the sooner that would pass.

A puff of thick blue smoke and the engine ticked over with a rumbling rattle. Power tremendously greater than usual lay at the touch of the throttle, the rest was a jumble of unaccustomed impressions: the rolling gait of the narrow undercarriage as I taxied out, the dropping wing and emphatic swing as the over-coarse fixed-pitch propeller laboriously gripped the air, dragging the machine into a run faster and longer than anything I had experienced before.

Trees on the far side of the aerodrome rose like a barrier with the aeroplane held on the ground by a wing-loading nearly twice as great as that of any previous fighter. It seemed impossible that we could lift in time – and yet it was too late to stop. The echoes of my thoughts recognised a situation encountered many times before. I moved back the control. The jolting ceased, and we were airborne with nose and wing blotting out the trees, unpleasantly close though they must be. Independent of my will, the Spitfire sailed into the sky.

For some minutes I held the controls quite still, before I groped against the heavy slipstream and closed the hood. The roar of the airflow receded, but within the confined cabin the racket of the engine grew threefold. Great waves of sound pounded my senses, as we climbed in a long, flat trajectory at an incredible speed compared with that of the Gladiator, the fastest biplane fighter of the day.

I tried to translate the meaning of the glowing green signal on the dashboard. Ah, the undercarriage! I found the actuating lever and pumped vigorously. The flight path oscillated violently with each stroke, for I could not stop my left hand on the control column from moving in sympathy. The longitudinal response seemed dangerously sensitive. For a moment I was apprehensive, but the thuds of the undercarriage legs locking into the wings reassured me with the explanation, and the machine settled into a steady flight path. Already the Spitfire's formidable personality was becoming part of my consciousness, and the slipstream hurrying past the flimsy hood epitomised the swift current of my thoughts. The thunder and din ceased to be recognisable as noise, and with an ever-recurrent trick of imagination turned into walls imprisoning me more strongly than the confines of the closefitting hood. I looked through the perspex at the broad fields, golden again with harvest, a background stage-drop, set for a solitary actor.

Suddenly a Gladiator appeared a thousand feet above, its fixed cantilever undercarriage extended towards me like an eagle's claws, and offering the opportunity of a mock dog-fight.

I drew the stick back in the manner to which I had been long accustomed, unprepared for the lightness of control.

A vice clamped my temples, my face muscles sagged, and all was blackness. My pull on the stick must have relaxed instantly, but even so, my returning vision found the Spitfire almost vertical and the Gladiator fully two thousand feet below.

More than a thousand flights since then with many versions of the Spitfire, which we manufactured under licence at Westland, have endeared it above all others of similar vintage.

Together we ventured into every kind of weather: clawing through dark clouds and bursting from pinnacle tops into dazzling sunlight; groping with throttled engine and dead radio above shadowed ground made featureless by breathless mist; flying in the suspense of the dark spears of tempestuous rain attacking the windscreen and obliterating all view. But there were calm days, too, of summer sun, and tall clouds drifting like great ships with glowing sails, days when the skies yearned with remembrance of peaceful years and forgot they had become the medium of war.

The sense of unfettered power made it almost impossible to fly this aeroplane without sweeping into the curves of aerobatic flight: the skies whirling under wing, the earth appearing in its stead and rolling over sideways, further and further, until once again sky and earth were in their appointed place. Power surged through the metal structure as the throttle was opened fully and the fighter lifted from its dive into a racing climb to a peak that displayed five counties in the same small panel of windscreen which a few seconds earlier had framed only fields. Into the far infinity of the skies I gazed. Was the enduring permanence of the earth-world designed merely to shelter the fleeting impermanence of men? What was the answer to the riddle of this universe in which man vainly and illogically dreamed himself king?

Soon to that same earth I hastened to return, the glory of the universe discarded for the sights and sounds with which life seeks to hide its loneliness and apprehension. Time and again, while the months mounted into years, the pattern of such flights was repeated with other types of fighters, both single-engined and twin. Always there was the closed-in solitude, thunderous noise, the rhythmic undercurrent of vibration, whirling propeller discs, the far-away patchwork of countryside indefinitely seen through cabin windows, or the obliteration of cloud thicker and more suffocating than fog.

Presently the heights would be attained: the symbol of mankind's endeavour, a wing frozen against the endless emptiness of the metallic blue and the white blaze of the sun.

In the illusory motionlessness of high flight I would poise, crouching and still, my own heartbeats fused with the aeroplane's vibrations, and the only tangibility the sun-filled cabin, its instruments covered with light hoarfrost. In that tumultuous noiselessness I was startled to hear suddenly in the earphones a voice: 'Hello Owlbird, this is Dogster. Please transmit for a fix.'

Each flight of this epoch now was worked into the pattern of a comprehensive system of ground control and radio aids; yet there were occasions when the plotting failed to differentiate between a hostile aeroplane and an allied one, and times when some airborne operation imposed radio silence.

On one such occasion early in the war I took a new-type twin-engined fighter, the Whirlwind, on test. Unbroken overcast at 10,000 feet sealed an all too limited sandwich of space between ground and sky for so fast a machine. Soon all that was possible at low altitude had been completed, so I radioed we were climbing to gain height above the strata for a dive. A brief, tenuous light, like smoke at the end of a tunnel, heralded our break through the clouds into the radiant blue above. I looked around. Barely half a mile away was another aeroplane flying an oblique intercept-ing course almost at my level. I banked away to avoid collision and levelling, glanced again at the intruder. With quick shock I saw black crosses. A Hun! There was no more than irony in the four cannon projecting aggressively from my own fighter: they held no ammunition because test pilots ranked as civilians and we would have broken the rules of war.

I put the nose down, plunging for the safety of cloud. Simultaneously the Me. 109, impressed by guns and twin engines, jerked into a steep turn away from me and dived for the same cloud cover. We entered it at the same moment, but in opposite direc-tions – and there I stayed a good ten minutes, for the first time in my life finding relief at flying blind.

When eventually the shadowed earth came to view it was dull and tired, as though bereft of hope at the futility of warring man. Yet as I looked around that subdued landscape, searching for the landmarks that would bring me home, I noted the first faint green of opening buds – and, dropping lower, sign upon sign of awakening spring. In my desire to escape, conviction insisted again and again that all that mat-tered was the safety of the earth, the essential earth in which is rooted every human aspiration; the earth that lets time spin by and discards the love of lovers, yet is always waiting to entrap newcomers to the world of love; the earth where I longed to live for today – tomorrow might not come.

11 W.E.W. Petter 1908–1968

Glyn Davies

An important event that occurred during the lead-up to the Westland Centenary was the publication of the book; Lysander to Lightning *by Professor Glyn Davies. The book was a long overdue biography of W.E.W. Petter. The aircraft he designed are renowned the world over, and yet his name is not generally recognised. The publication of Glyn's book fills a void and gives Petter his place in history.*

The names of R.J. Mitchell and Sydney Camm, designers of the Spitfire and Hurricane fighters, are as legendary as are their aircraft. The name of 'Teddy' Petter is almost unknown today, and yet his aircraft types are more numerous, more radical in design, and as familiar. The Lysander, Whirlwind, Welkin, Canberra, Lightning and Gnat were all innovative: nothing like them had been designed before (or after).

Teddy Petter came from an illustrious family of engineers in the West Country. His great grandfather John Petter developed a prosperous ironmongery in Barnstable and was able to buy for his son James a business: Iron Mongers of Yeovil. James was clearly an adventurous engineer and was able to buy out the Yeovil Foundry and Engineering works. He designed a high-quality, open-fired grate called the Nautilus which became famous after being selected by Queen Victoria for installation in Balmoral Castle and Osborne House in the Isle of Wight.

James had fifteen children, the fourth and fifth of these being the twins Percival Waddams and Ernest Willoughby, the latter of whom became Teddy's father. Percival was the talented engineer, designing and building over a thousand engines for agricultural use. Teddy's father, Ernest, believed his talents were in entrepreneurial business, and he worked hard at becoming part of the London establishment. (In 1925 he was knighted for organising the engineering section of the British Empire Exhibition.)

In 1915 Lloyd George exposed the inadequacy of Britain's aircraft industry for continuing the war. Ernest and Percival rushed to the Admiralty, offering their facilities and expertise for the war effort. The result was that they received a subcontract to produce seaplanes for Short Bros, and this led to the foundation of the Westland factory and airfield. During the war Westland built over one thousand biplanes.

Teddy was born in 1908 and at the age of 12 his father sent him to Marlborough to have his character formed through rugby and cricket. He did not enjoy sport but became an outstanding scholar, going on to Cambridge where he obtained a first-class honours in the Mechanical Tripos and a gold medal in Aerodynamics. On graduating in 1929 he agreed to his father's suggestion that he join Westland as a 'graduate apprentice' spending two years moving through the shops. Teddy would say later that he looked on this as sheer drudgery but admitted that without workshop knowledge he would never have become a designer.

In 1934 Sir Ernest announced that Teddy would be co-opted to the board and assumed the title of Technical Director at the age of 26, with the Chief Designer Arthur Davenport (age 43) reporting to him! From the very beginning he conscientiously went around the design offices talking to, and advising on, aerodynamics, stress and weights. This practice he kept up all his working life and was consequently never taken by surprise when the unexpected arose.

Initially he worked with Davenport, but then after only a year Sir Ernest convened a shareholders' meeting to seek capital by merging with British Marine Aircraft. Teddy threatened to resign so it was decided not to proceed.

The first design for which Teddy was fully responsible, in response to a Government specification, was the Lysander, an aeronautical jeep, for which he had doubts on the need, and spent a great deal of time talking to pilots on this type of aircraft, before embarking on its production. The aircraft was not a success since the German Messerschmitt fighters had a much superior performance. However, the short-take-off-and-landing Lysander became famous for taking agents to occupied France and bringing them back. His second aircraft, the Whirlwind, was a two-engined fighter, faster than the Spitfire and carrying four lethal cannons, but was let down at altitude by its engines. The next aircraft, the Welkin, was a 'larger' Whirlwind but Petter underestimated the effects of compressibility at high Mach numbers (his only real technical error).

Meanwhile, Sir Ernest had negotiated a deal with John Brown Shipbuilders to take over Westland Aircraft, and appoint Eric Mensforth (who knew nothing about aircraft) as Managing Director. Teddy was furious and saw the loss of family control as the loss of his birthright. He even reported adversely on his father's conduct to the Air Ministry, but no wrongdoing was discovered. Clashes between Teddy and Eric Mensforth seemed inevitable.

Throughout his career Teddy was known to take off from work for a period of up to six weeks or so, without warning, at times of stress or frustration. He was deeply religious and it was believed he fled to a monastery or religious commune, and returned refreshed and bristling with ideas. On one occasion, when he was looking at possible high-speed bombers, he disappeared for six weeks, returning to find that Mensforth had put the entire project office to work on a naval fighter, the Wyvern. Teddy was furious and resigned immediately.

Petter had by now become well known and admired at the Ministry of Aircraft Production, so it was fairly straightforward for him to approach senior Government advisers, in particular Sir George Nelson, who was able to offer him the post of Chief Engineer at English Electric. This firm had been able to produce Halifax bombers at the astonishing rate of one a day in 1942, but had no design capability. Petter immediately did two things. Firstly, he recruited the best team of engineers, which eventually became the most successful aircraft designers in Europe for over half a century. Secondly, he designed his most successful aircraft, the Canberra. This aircraft was designed to a Government specification for a very fast high-altitude bomber which needed no armament. Petter's design looked pedestrian compared to, say, the swept wing B-47, but it had an extraordinary manoeuvrability for a bomber. It so impressed the Americans that 400 were built under licence by Glenn Martin. It smashed countless world records for distance and time, and for altitude. Another radical aircraft was the supersonic Lightning fighter, which had thin wings swept at 60^0, and generated lift at take-off the same way as did Concorde, years later!

During the development of the two aircraft, Petter had continuous arguments with Arthur Sheffield, the head of production at Preston. Petter wished to be in charge of all experimental and development stages at Warton, with the flexibility to act quickly as problems arose. Sheffield felt he had all the standards of quality control to implement. Matters came to a head when the Ministry ordered three varieties of the Canberra, and Sheffield blamed Petter for the resulting chaos. Petter appealed to Sir George, who declined to back him, so he resigned immediately. Pleas from all of his team to 'continue the fight' were to no avail.

For most of the year 1950, Petter probably brooded on the lessons learned at English Electric, in particular the capital cost of England's first supersonic fighter, and the even higher cost of keeping such a complicated machine in service. (More Lightnings were out of service than in, at any given time.) Coincidentally, the company founded by Henry Folland was looking for an opportunity to design and make, instead of just subcontract, work which it had been doing for twenty years.

Petter was invited to join Follands as a Technical Drector and Managing Director Designate, pending the retirement of Henry Folland due to ill health. Petter accepted and immediately set about recruiting a design team to produce a lightweight fighter. Such was the loyalty he inspired that some half a dozen senior engineers from English Electric moved to join him. In three years his aircraft the Midge flew, and impressed countless test pilots, from the RAF, Indian Air force, Canada, New Zealand, Jordan and the USAAF. An American pilot went so far as to say 'you don't have to climb into this aircraft, you put it on'.

The next aircraft he designed was a larger version, the Gnat, with the new engine, the Bristol Orpheus. This light aircraft (one third the weight and cost) had an amazing performance, and inspired the Americans to support a NATO requirement for a simple European aircraft, to be built in large numbers, and be able to take off from 'cow pastures' the Russians would be incapable of finding and destroying.

The Gnat in 1954 would have a two-year lead on any other European contenders, but no one, including Stanley Hooker the Orpheus designer, had allowed for Petter's obstinacy. He refused to alter his fuselage to enable low-pressure tyres to be fitted. Consequently the design was awarded to Fiat, with a larger machine which first flew in 1956! His design was eventually accepted by the Government in the form of the Gnat two-seat trainer, which was adopted by the RAF and became famous as a mount for their 'Red Arrows'.

This design was Petter's last. Follands was ordered by the Government to join Hawker Siddeley, but Petter could never work for Sydney Camm, so he resigned for the last time.

In 1959 his beloved wife Claude started to show signs of Parkinson's disease, for which there was no cure. Petter and Claude heard of a Father Forget in France, a defrocked priest, who claimed to be a faith healer. Teddy, his wife, and young daughter joined Forget in his commune, never to return to England. The 'father' took every penny of their savings and separated the family in order that they could give their undivided attention to the Lord. Petter eventually died in 1968. Claude died seven years later.

Bespectacled Teddy was blessed with a classical intellect and appearance, deceiving newcomers, especially Government officials, who might think he was a pushover. Although basically shy he was always convinced of his own judgement, he gave no quarter in battles with colleagues, or officials, and he was nearly always right. How he managed to be taken in by a religious charlatan remains a mystery. We will never see his like again.

12 The Bombing of Yeovil

Dilip Sarkar

Yeovil suffered a number of air attacks during the Second World War, hardly surprising, being as it was involved in the production of Spitfires and Seafires. Neighbouring Sherborne was also badly hit in a separate raid as part of the same onslaught.

Dilip Sarkar relates the full tale in his book Angriff Westland.

For the populace of Yeovil, *Lord Haw Haw*'s malicious warning became harsh reality on Monday, 7 October 1940.

At 15.45 that afternoon when the *Alert* wailed Yeovil's thirty-third air-raid warning of the war, haunted by the spectre of Sherborne's recent agony, people took notice and sought shelter immediately. In what was also Yeovil's first experience of bombing, the first bombs are reported as having fallen at 15.55. All fell in the town centre, causing damage and loss of life at Montague Burton's store in Middle Street, St Andrew's Road, and Summerleaze Park. Direct hits were also recorded on shelters at the Methodist Church in Vicarage Street and at 45 Grove Avenue. An engineering firm, Ricketts Ltd in Belmont Street, and nearby houses were also seriously damaged. The final civilian death toll would be sixteen, with nine others seriously wounded and twenty less so.

Mrs Margaret Hewlett:

'My husband and I were in Woolworth's at the time, next-door to Burton's menswear shop where there was a direct hit. Eight people were killed there. The whole front of Woolworth's was blown in, but, fortunately we had both moved back from the front of the store. There were several people injured and a lot of panic as a gas main had burst. We all tried to get out by the back

entrance and as quickly as possible. The Emergency Services did a good job, though, and the fire was soon under control.'

Fred Denham:

'*The bombs on Burton's and the billiard hall above it fell just 150 yards from my First Aid Post. A bomb had exploded on the steps between there and Woolworth's where many were sheltering. I ran there carrying a stretcher with another chap. We got two women from the top of the steps but the others were all dead. We did what we could for various people but swiftly moved on to the Methodist Church in nearby Vicarage Street where a shelter had been hit.*'

John Chesterman:

'*I remember seeing a tremendous fighter escort flying around the bombers overhead.*'

Henry Smith:

'*My elder brother, Albert, was employed at the time at the Southern Railway Station in Yeovil and was in bed following a night shift. My mother and I were in the farm cottage where we lived at Brympton D'Evercy. Suddenly we heard the siren followed by explosions from falling bombs. My brother got up and the three of us took shelter in a ditch at the bottom of the garden. In the adjacent field a barrage balloon was sited with two huts housing the crew, I suppose about three miles from the airfield. It would appear that one of the aircraft had overshot the target and dropped its bombs near us. An oil bomb was dropped in the ditch where we sheltered. Fortunately the ditch was dog legged which sheltered us from the blast. Another bomb, an HE, fell in front of the barrage balloon hut. Following the bombing the NCO in charge came running to look for us at the damaged cottage and said that one of his men was missing. Then the displaced earth at the edge of the crater moved and out stepped the "missing" man, shaken but otherwise unhurt!*'

Once again, however, Westland miraculously remained unscathed.

13 The Good Neighbour

Graham Mottram

The Royal Naval Air Station at Yeovilton (HMS Heron) was built at the beginning of the Second World War, and is situated only a few miles to the north of the Yeovil factory.

It has been a major base for the Fleet Air Arm since 1940 and has remained a large and very active military airfield since that time, close enough to affect 'A Quiet Country Town'.

For many years Westland maintained a site there, mainly concerned with their fixed-wing commitments.

The following item is an extract from 'Yeovilton' by Cdr P.M. Rippon and Graham Mottram, published for the Fleet Air Arm Museum in 1990.

Westland senior foreman Fred Walker first remembers Yeovilton on a July afternoon in 1940, when he was ordered to 'Get on out to Ilchester' and meet Lord Aberconway who would be arriving to view the new site. Well, he knew where Ilchester was and eventually found Westland's new factory, just in time to see Lord Aberconway arrive with his entourage of Westland senior management, one of whom took him on one side and said, 'We know you don't know anything about this, Walker, so if he asks any questions just let us do the talking.'

Lord Aberconway, who in 1938 had replaced Sir Ernest Petter as chairman of Westland, marched the length of the hangar and once round the paint shop, then without saying a word, got back into his car, and the party left. Fred was just wondering what to do next, when an aeroplane dropped out of the cloud, and deposited its bombs on the nearby airfield. That was his introduction to what was to be his workplace for the next twelve years.

The Westland hangar at Yeovilton was set on the south side of the bend in Pyle Lane, about 400ft long by 100ft wide, with offices at the eastern end, overlooking the workshop floor. Large sliding doors along the hangar's south side led out onto a concrete apron and aircraft park, from which a gateway gave access to the airfield on the other side of Pyle Lane.

Here, two further hangars were designated for Westland use during the war, but later reverted to Yeovilton's Station flight. One of them has since been demolished. A handful of experienced workers were transferred from Yeovil and Miss Young, the Women's Supervisor, was instructed to take on all the girls she could to supplement the work force. For training, every man had a mate, and the mate was a girl; that idea was popular.

Being on a naval air station, it is tempting to suppose that Westland were converting ex-RAF aircraft into naval types, but in fact this was never done at Yeovilton, but the majority of the work was rebuilding RAF Spitfires, interspersed with other urgent contracts on some of Westland's own marks. One of these contracts was to strip down Lysanders ready for crating and shipment to Malta. These were wanted so urgently that they were flown straight into Yeovilton and stripped down in the salvage hangar (on the other side of Pyle Lane). Any bad girls used to be sent over to the salvage department, as it was considered to be a horrible job!

Another contract involving Lysanders was their conversion for secret operations in occupied Europe. This meant fitting a 'Harrow' long-range tank under the fuselage, and installing special radio equipment. The aircraft also had to be painted matt black, and a ladder fixed to the side. The ladder had to have a couple of luminous patches so that an agent waiting on the ground could find it easily in the dark, and climb aboard the slowly moving aircraft.

RAF pilots of Westland Whirlwind fighters would sometimes fly straight to Yeovilton for running repairs after being shot up. The Westland team would swing into action while the pilot waited, and as soon as the work was finished he would give it a quick test flight around the airfield, and if it was considered to be satisfactory he would waggle his wings and disappear into the blue. On at least one occasion this practice aroused the wrath of the naval Commander (Flying), who complained it was setting a bad example for his trainee pilots.

Test flying of Westland's normal Yeovilton output was supposed to be done by Westland's own pilots, and they too occasionally fell foul of naval displeasure. Chief test pilot, Harald Penrose, certainly disliked being ordered about by the Navy, and would avoid working from Yeovilton if he could, leaving most of the Yeovilton flying to Jimmy Ramsden. In wartime the Yeovilton factory came under the jurisdiction of the Civilian Repair Organisation, and when the CRO phoned up one day to ask if there were any planes ready, they were told there were several waiting for flying. 'What do you mean, waiting for flying?' 'Well, we can't get anybody up from Yeovil; they're all too busy.' 'Never mind your main works, you ring us when the planes are ready, and we'll send you pilots to fly them.' Although this was contrary to Westland's contract, it was all eventually sorted out over a lunch at the Manor Hotel.

As the war came to an end, Yeovilton's Westland hangar had very little work. Eventually the Air Ministry rang up the main works and said, 'We must keep your Yeovilton unit going, and we're prepared, if you can send somebody up, to give you a refurbishing contract on 150 Spitfires.' So, Fred Walker was despatched with Bill Samways, the chief inspector, to move around the squadrons to have a look at these Spitfires. At RAF Cosford, which was a 'spit and polish' sort of station, they were shown a chart on the wall, showing all the stages of the job, totalling 180 hours. Having seen the aircraft, our Westland friends were a bit sceptical, but the Ministry said they were only prepared to pay for 180 hours on each Spitfire. The Spitfires were flown into Yeovilton, where Westland made the best of a bad job, but the first ones they delivered back to Cosford were rejected. According to Fred Walker, 'There were loads of things wanted doing, but we didn't do them, because they only wanted us to do 180 hours work on them.' What RAF Cosford had neglected to tell everyone about their 180 hour chart, was that if they found any damage they would take the plane out of the line, and it could be out for a month, while they were doing repairs on it, and then they would bring it back and carry on with the 180 hours. Finally the Ministry agreed that Westland could have the contract on a cost plus system.

By now the Spitfires were declining into second-line duties, as jet fighters took over the air defence role. The Gloster Meteor had been the first jet to enter operational service in 1944, but the maximum operating height of the improved post-war versions was limited by pilot discomfort in the Meteor's unpressurised cockpit. Westland had gained valuable experience of pressurising cockpits during the development of the wartime high-altitude fighter, the Westland Welkin, and the company was awarded a contract to modify the cockpits of about thirty Meteor F4s. The aircraft were modified in the Yeovilton hangar and this work, along with the Spitfire contract, kept the operation going until 1952. The workforce had been reduced since the war years. Most of the female workers had already left, but now finding work became a real problem, with talk of making electric irons and the like, it was time for the old hands to leave.

The parent company had by now made the move into helicopter construction, and a few Service Dragonflies and Whirlwinds trickled in to keep the refurbishment operations going. Another major contract for jet fighters was obtained in 1956, both the Gloster Meteor and its contemporary, the de Havilland Vampire, were 'straight-winged' jets, a feature which limited their maximum speed. Warsaw Pact countries were already using the swept-wing MiG-15, which had outflown the Meteors it had met in combat over Korea. The North American Sabre (F86E) had proved equal to the MiG during the Korean War, and it was the only swept-wing fighter available to NATO forces for the Defence of Western Europe. Funded by the USA under the Mutual Defence Aid Programme, the RAF obtained 430 Sabres built by Canadair, delivered in 1952/3. When the Hawker Hunter finally became available in 1955/6, the Sabres were released by the RAF, which contracted with Westland for their refurbishment. The Sabres were turned out of Yeovilton in USAF markings, and test flown from Yeovilton or Merryfield before being handed back to the Americans. Most of them were then transferred under MDAP arrangements to other European countries, predominantly Italy and Yugoslavia.

By this time the company was wholly into helicopters, and their refurbishments, Dragonflies, Whirlwinds and latterly Wessex, kept Yeovilton's hangar busy for many years. Many of Yeovilton's sailors were fascinated by the apparition 'parked' behind the hangar in the late 1960s, the Westland Westminster 'sky crane' helicopter, a project which never progressed beyond two prototypes.

Fixed-wing aircraft returned as a result of Westland having taken over Fairey Aviation in 1960, and the refurbishment of Fairey Gannets occupied much of the workforce. A Gannet was the last aircraft to leave the Yeovilton hangar in 1975, when the refurbishment operation was transferred to Weston-super-Mare. From then until 1985, when the Royal Navy purchased the hangar, Westland Yeovilton was a component repair facility, working on items such as wiring looms and hydraulic systems to support the main Yeovil factory. After a substantial rebuilding, the hangar returned to housing Westland products, the Wessex and Sea King helicopters of 707 Squadron.

14 Normalair

Mike Bednall

As aircraft companies develop it often becomes apparent that there is an underlying interest in some aspect of their activity. In the case of Westland this turned out to be one of cabin conditioning. As early as 1917 the Westland Weasel, two-seat fighter included electrical heating and an oxygen system, and later with the flight over the summit of Everest in 1933.

The need for aircraft, capable of prolonged operation at high altitudes, emerged again during the Second World War.

The Westland response had a far-reaching effect at Yeovil, as compiled by Mike Bednall.

From the very beginning there seemed to be a culture of understanding within the design staff at Westland that crew comfort played an important part in combat effectiveness. A heating system for the crew was provided as part of the design for the Weasel two-seat fighter.

This interest arose again when Westland was involved in the expedition to fly over the summit of Everest. Here the problem was not only temperature but the rarefied atmosphere above 30,000 feet.

The Westland designers set about designing an effective oxygen system. The flight over Everest would not only entail prolonged operation of the aircraft in demanding flight conditions but a considerable amount of physical work on the part of the observer/photographer. A simple demand system was built in with four 750-litre capacity cylinders, the fourth of which would be considered for emergency only.

The crew used heated suits and much of the equipment which was also sensitive to temperature required heating; the result was that a robust electrical heating system was built into the aircraft.

There can be little doubt that the effectiveness of the system was a contributory factor in the success and safety of the expedition.

By 1940, the world was at war and aircraft capable of operations in the stratosphere (above 30,000ft) were available to both sides. Following the Battle of Britain the Luftwaffe was quick to appreciate the protection offered by altitude for reconnaissance, and by 1941 enemy aircraft was constantly penetrating deep into Britain immune from attack. As early as 1938, work had been in hand to develop pressurisation systems, mainly undertaken by Vickers-Armstrong with the Wellington V and VI.

Specification F.4/40 was issued in July 1940, calling for a twin-engined High Altitude Fighter and Westland responded with the P.14 Welkin, a very large machine powered by two Rolls-Royce Merlins, with four 20mm cannon and a pressure cabin that would allow operations as high as 40,000ft. The overall configuration was similar to that of the Whirlwind fighter, but the Welkin was as large as the Whirlwind was small. It had a wingspan of 70ft and the overall dimensions were in proportion, except that the high-aspect ratio wing was clearly intended to sustain the aircraft in the rarefied atmosphere in which it was intended to operate. Another feature of the design was the clear bubble canopy, coupled with the short nose designed to allow maximum all around observation during the interception phase.

The Welkin test programme was pursued with energy, and by 1944 was in production at Yeovil. Over 100 aircraft were produced or in an advanced state of build before it was accepted that the high-altitude threat had passed.

Westland were quick to appreciate that the stratosphere would be the realm of the jet fighter and bomber, and that the experience and understanding they had gained gave them a commercial edge over their competitors.

Westland's Chief Experimental Engineer, Bill Widgery, had been working for some time on a cabin pressure control valve, which he described as a 'leaking altimeter'; it had subsequently been tested in a modified Spitfire, these early tests showing sufficient promise to embark upon the design of a specialised control valve to maintain a desired cabin altitude. The Westland Control Valve, as it became known, was at the heart of the cabin conditioning for the Welkin, and the prototype flew for the first time in November 1942.

In the latter half of 1944 it became clear that the war would be over and if companies were to survive in the post-war world, it would be necessary to develop aircraft for the civil market. Five years of war had developed aircraft capable of much higher speeds and able to operate continuously at higher altitude. The military transport aircraft already in worldwide service with the Allied Forces would clearly form the basis for future airliners and it was obvious that technical advances around the corner would quickly place a demand for operation at 30,000 feet or above.

The Westland cabin control valve was already incorporated in a number of military aircraft, but many of the manufacturers involved were beginning to express doubts, having placed orders with Westland who could be a full competitor.

Thus it was that Westland formed a separate company in June 1946, under the name of Normalair. The whole of Normalair's facilities were situated within the Westland Aircraft complex, with no specific isolation between the two Companies.

The new company dominated the market quickly, to become the UK specialists in cabin atmosphere control.

In the late 1940s Westland and Normalair met Garrett AiResearch of the USA as defendants in a legal case alleging infringements of Boeing patents on cabin pressurisation technique. Agreement was reached, including the first of many licence agreements with Garrett in 1947. Although it has now generally been accepted that there was no infringement of the Garrett and Boeing patents, this episode nevertheless established a close association between Garrett and Normalair.

This was not only important for the extension of Normalair's products and business, but it also eventually resulted in the Garrett Corporation obtaining a 48 per cent shareholding in the company.

With the aid of Garrett licences and through its own development efforts, Normalair's cabin pressurisation and air conditioning activities grew vigorously, and there were soon very few European civil or military aircraft in the 1950s which did not have Normalair equipment fitted.

Meanwhile in 1949, with the advent of the jet engine making it possible for military aircraft to operate at altitudes of 50,000ft or more, the UK authorities decided to make demand oxygen systems mandatory.

In the USA, demand oxygen regulators based on captured German designs were available with the result that Ministry of Aviation and Supply encouraged Normalair to approach an American manufacturer. In 1951 an agreement was signed with Bendix for Normalair to modify and manufacture the Bendix D 1 demand regulator to meet UK requirements. In all, some 50,000 regulators of various marks based on the Bendix D 1 were produced by Normalair.

Further extensions of the Bendix licence enabled Normalair to develop and manufacture liquid oxygen (LOX) converters as well as regulators. Then in the early 1950s the Royal Aircraft Establishment chose to pass the responsibility for all military oxygen work to Normalair, as a result of which the company acquired complete life support systems capability, including masks and emergency oxygen supplies.

Whilst Normalair was developing a complete environmental conditioning and life support systems capability, further diversification of its product range took place. In 1960 agreements with Bendix brought the licensed production of hydraulic servo valves into the product range. Hydraulics expertise was then developed for electro-hydraulic servo valves, actuators and the very successful lightweight solenoid-operated hydraulic valves. Further agreements with Bendix gave Normalair the entree into marine hydraulics, especially for submarine applications. By the 1980s, the range of aerospace hydraulic products covered most of the airframe utility hydraulics, including selector valves, manifolds, accumulators and reservoirs.

As the Normalair Company grew, the association with the Garrett Corporation became stronger, and in 1967 the Garrett Corporation obtained a 48 per cent shareholding, Westland plc retaining a 52 per cent majority holding. It was at this point that the company name was changed to Normalair-Garrett Limited (NGL).

The progressive growth of NGL was achieved by a vigorous policy of new product development, and by the acquisition of other companies and technologies. In 1971 NGL acquired Teddington Aircraft Controls, a UK Company with a complementary range of aircraft environmental equipment, which consolidated NGL as the European leader in this field.

A range of electromechanical actuators, de-icing equipment, pressure switches and hot air valves were introduced to NGL's range of products through this acquisition.

The broadening of NGL's product range and the need to support a wide range of products operating worldwide necessitated the setting up, in 1971, of the self-sufficient Product Support Division at Bournemouth. This organisation was required to provide a reliable after-sales, repair, overhaul and test facility as well as spares and technical publications for all NGL products. The resultant growth of NGL's product support business necessitated a move to larger and more suitable premises. At the beginning of 1986 a new, dedicated facility was opened at Hurn Airport, which included a comprehensive range of test facilities, the intention being to minimise dependence on the production test facilities at Yeovil.

In 1971 NGL brought A.M. Fell of Newhaven and Aircraft Supplies Limited of Bournemouth, and with these purchases acquired a great deal of flight recorder technology. The 'Midas' crash recorder then in widespread use in British airlines was also acquired. This flight recorder technology was complementary to the industrial data loggers and energy monitoring systems which NGL had taken over from Saunders-Roe during the mergers and rationalisations in the Westland Group in 1959 and 1960. It was also becoming evident that electronics was becoming increasingly involved in aircraft environmental control systems, and so a self-supporting Electronics Division was set up on a new site in Yeovil in 1979, to consolidate all the company's electronic activities into a single unit. It was to provide a centre of competence in applying advanced electronic technology to energy management and industrial applications, in addition to satisfying the demanding requirements of aerospace, marine and defence systems. NGL's greatest success was the development and production of the miniature maintenance data tape recorder for the American F-18 aircraft. Further developments of higher-capacity recorders and solid-state recorders ensured that NGL remained in the forefront of the aerospace recording business.

The company's increasing requirement for high-quality precision castings led to the formation of a Foundry Division at Chard in 1972, and later a second foundry was set up in Singapore. These divisions manufactured lost-wax investment castings using ferrous, nickel, cobalt, copper and aluminium-based alloys.

A major advancement in high-strength castings was achieved by developing double-vacuum-melting maraging steel castings for aerospace applications.

For many years NGL had been a user of filters which were incorporated in the various NGL system product lines. In 1976 a licence agreement with Facet Enterprises in the USA, to manufacture a range of aircraft, marine and industrial filters, was transferred from Vokes Limited to NGL. This range was expanded by NGL with new filter designs for numerous applications including hydraulic, lubrication, fuel and gas systems. The filters were produced by the Filtration Division of NGL and marketed worldwide.

In April 1979, Westland plc purchased the whole of the share capital of Westlake Aeromarine Engines Limited (WAEL) and appointed NGL to manage their affairs. The association of WAEL with NGL was further enhanced by the additional technical and management resources which were available at the headquarters division of NGL at Yeovil.

As a consequence WAEL became the Propulsion Division of NGL and developed a small gas turbine for ground and airborne applications. WAEL piston engines were used in a wide range of target drones such as the Skeet and Banshee and were also selected for the GEC/Flight Refuelling Phoenix RPV being procured for the British Army. In a sense, the wheel turned full circle with the manufacture of engines at Yeovil once again, Westland having been set up on the original Petters Engine site.

The Ordnance Division was set up in 1980 on a new site at Crewkerne to cater for the volume production of weapon equipment using highly automated manufacturing techniques. The country's first flexible manufacturing system (FMS) was set up to produce the light duty ejector release unit, or weapon rack, for the Tornado aircraft. At the same time, a design and development facility for weapon control systems was set up on the site. High-performance missile and smart sub-munition actuation systems using cold gas, hot gas, electric and hydraulic energy sources were developed within this facility.

In 1981 NGL acquired Delaney Galley Dynamics Limited to strengthen the in-house capability for the manufacture of heat exchangers to complement NGL's thirty years' experience in the use of such products. A useful spin-off was the capability to fabricate very lightweight structures using the salt-bath and vacuum brazing techniques used for making heat exchangers.

The development of molecular sieve oxygen concentrators was seen to provide a considerable increase in market potential for life support equipment and so, in 1983, the Life Support Division was formed, based in Yeovil, to build on the advantages arising out of the winning of major contracts from the USA for the supply of On-Board Oxygen Generation Systems.

In 1986, the Signal Group of companies which included Garrett merged with the Allied Group which includes Bendix to form Allied Signal Inc. Thus, the two principal licensors from which much of NGL's core technology was developed came together with NGL as part of one family.

Forty years on, NGL has grown steadily from its small beginnings into a sizeable company with over 2,000 employees and a turnover exceeding £70 million. Although aircraft environmental conditioning still forms by far the greatest proportion of its business, a policy of horizontal broadening into other technologies complementary to existing product lines has enabled a wide range of product groups to be developed. NGL's growth took place primarily within its own market area, aerospace, by opportunism. Then gradual movement into army and navy areas took place, together with NGL exposure to other government departments, and hence to the nationalised utilities.

NGL has long been involved in international programmes, starting with the Transall, and, by winning appreciable business on the tri-national Tornado and in America on the F-18 and BI-B programmes, has proved itself capable of meeting the increasingly competitive demands of tomorrow's multinational aircraft programmes.

In 1985, Allied merged with the Signal Companies, adding critical mass to its aerospace, automotive and engineered materials businesses. Founded by Sam Mosher in 1922 as the Signal Gasoline Company, Signal was originally a California company that produced gasoline from natural gas. In 1928, the company changed its name to Signal Oil & Gas, entering into oil production the same year. Signal merged with the Garrett Corporation, a Los Angeles-based aerospace company, and in 1968 adopted the Signal Companies as its corporate name.

The addition of Signal's Garrett division to Bendix made aerospace Allied-Signal's largest business sector. In 1985, the company sold 50 per cent of Union Texas, and in 1986 it divested thirty-five non-strategic businesses through the formation and spin-off of The Henley Group, Inc.

In mid-1991, with a new CEO, Lawrence A. Bossidy, and new leadership in many key businesses, Allied-Signal began a comprehensive programme of transformation. Bold actions were taken to improve cash flow and operating margins, to increase productivity, and to position the company as a global competitive force for the years ahead. The Allied-Signal name was changed to AlliedSignal in 1993 to reinforce a one-company image and signify the full integration of all of its businesses. In 1992, the company sold its remaining interest in Union Texas through a public offering for $940 million in net proceeds.

Throughout the 1990s, Lawrence A. Bossidy led a growth and productivity transformation that quintupled the market value of AlliedSignal shares and significantly outperformed the Dow Jones Industrial Average and the S&P 500.

15 Helicopters

O.L.L. Fitzwilliams

The prolific output of fixed-wing aircraft from the Westland factory took place over the period 1915–55, little more than one third of the century we are now celebrating.

The decision to change emphasis, and to specialise in helicopters, was without doubt a 'defining moment', and a bold decision. The practical helicopter that could be produced in quantity and operated commercially had only been in existence for little over five years, and its future was by no means clear. The Westland board decided that rather than attempt to enter the market with a design of their own, they would try to acquire an agreement to build an established design under licence.

Responsibility for the helicopter design office was placed with O.L.L. Fitzwilliams, who had worked with Raoul Hafner. He describes the process whereby Westland became a helicopter company in a publication originally produced by another rotorcraft pioneer, Reggie Brie.

After the war Westland were anxious to enter the civil market and they made a number of design studies of some civil aeroplanes (one closely resembling the later De Havilland Heron). However, a new civil aeroplane design would have interfered with their other commitments, and their attention was also very favourably attracted by the civil prospects of the helicopter.

The Chairman and others visited the United States with a view to arranging a licence for the construction in England of an American helicopter. Prior to this they took advice from many quarters, including from myself when I was in charge of the Rotary Wing Section at Beaulieu.

My advice favoured Sikorsky, which coincided with their own inclinations, and in December 1946 Westland signed a Licence Agreement with Sikorsky for the construction in England of an anglicised version of the S-51, later to be known under the name Dragonfly given to it by the Royal Navy.

Due to a complete prohibition on dollar content, and the then wide differences between British and American materials and accessories, particularly bearings, the anglicising of the S-51 design was very extensive, every part of the British helicopter being in some respects (and many parts, in very major respects) different from the American original.

The magnitude of this task was greatly underrated and it was carried out by a tiny staff – there being only 14 people, including the secretary and office boy, in the department when the first Westland S-51 flew at the beginning of October, 1948.

I arrived at Yeovil in March 1947 but for a long period I was entirely isolated, and employed my time perfecting some notes, originally derived from Hafner at Sherburn-in-Elmet, which were later used by McClements as a basis for his 1948 lecture on rotor limitations.

The only other two persons at that time engaged on the S-51 were Mr Yates and Mr Pouncey (the latter of Jig & Tool Department) both of whom were with Sikorsky arranging for the transfer of drawings and technical data. The drawings finally arrived toward the end of May 1947, i.e. the first Westland S-51 flew approximately sixteen months after work actually started.

In principle, each American drawing issued to the works was accompanied by an auxiliary Westland drawing or 'Extract Sheet' containing instructions for anglicising the part. In practice, many of these 'Extract Sheets' were as complex as the American originals and even for the basic aircraft many of the drawings issued were Westland originals, as were all drawings for role equipment and other adaptations of the design.

The same scheme was initially used also for the Whirlwind for which nearly half the drawings were Westland originals, but in the end all Whirlwind 'Extract Sheets' were redrawn to conform with the standard SBAC drawing procedure.

A batch of 30 Westland-Sikorsky S-51s (this remained Ministry of Aviation official designation for this aircraft though it was later commonly known as the Dragonfly) were built entirely as a private speculation, and mostly using very provisional tooling, so that when military orders were later received, a gap of nearly eighteen months occurred while production tooling was provided.

Also the Drawing Office staff began to grow at this point, mainly to cover the installation of military equipment and the design of the many variations of this aircraft, which subsequently went into production.

Production of the Dragonfly was preceded in 1947 by the import of six Sikorsky, built S-51s which were used by us and by British European Airways and others on experimental services. One of these was of historical interest in that it was the first helicopter after Focke to carry an external load suspended from a point beneath the aircraft. Ignoring urgent Sikorsky advice to the contrary, Mr Yates and I designed the necessary lifting beam one Sunday, using as a guide a photograph of the lifting beam originally fitted to the Focke Fa 223. This equipment was used about a week later in the first public demonstration of external load lifting at Hampden Park Stadium in Glasgow (Spring 1948). During the history of the S-51 it underwent many changes, including the introduction of metal blades and powered controls plus droop locks for shipboard operation in addition to the airframe and engine changes.

The success of the Dragonfly led to another private venture in the building of the Westland S-55 (Whirlwind); some preliminary investigation had started in June 1950 and the Licence Agreement was announced by Westland in November 1950. At this time I remember receiving the strongest assurances from certain Ministry personnel that the Government had no intention whatever of buying this aircraft. Nevertheless, work proceeded and the first Whirlwind flew in November 1952.

The British services did acquire the Whirlwind in substantial numbers for use by the forces in a number of roles, including: Search and Rescue, Anti-submarine, Commando and Troop Carrying and VIP transport (including operation by 'The Queen's Flight').

As the design was upgraded to meet new requirements, the introduction of an R-R 'Gnome' gas turbine was undertaken.

A total of 364 Whirlwinds were built between 1953 and 1966, some 70 of which were for export customers.

Westland had done several studies of anti-submarine helicopters, but up to about 1955 the Ministry made it perfectly clear that the anti-submarine task had been allocated to the Bristol Company and that there was no interest in any Westland proposal.

The Wessex came into existence as the result of the emergency created by the cancellation of the Bristol 191, as a result of which the Ministry asked for an immediate Westland solution to the problem of providing the Navy with a suitable anti-submarine helicopter.

Westland thinking up to that time had assumed a twin-engined arrangement for this role, which was not favoured because of its novelty and the very short time scale available. However, by a remarkable coincidence, the Napier Gazelle had a few weeks previously passed a Type Test at 1250hp and this made it possible for Westland to propose the installation of this engine in an anglicised Sikorsky S-58 as suitable for the Navy's needs. The initial experimental installation of a Gazelle in a Sikorsky-built S-58 first flew in May 1957.

It is of interest that the original anti-submarine role envisaged for the Wessex (presumably derived from the requirement for the Type 191) did not require the automatic 'come-to-the-hover' manoeuvre. Consequently, the Wessex Mk.1, like the earlier Whirlwind Mk.7, was originally provided with automatic stabilisation, plus a simple autopilot, and could achieve automatic hover once the sonar was in the water, with direct manual control of engine power.

This simple version handled very well indeed and had the remarkable property that a pilot standing on the ground beside a cold Wessex took less than 30 seconds to climb into the aircraft, start it up and leave the ground. Much later in the programme, when several early Wessex were already flying, the requirement for an automatic flight control system was introduced, and the ability of the Westland team to get this (Sikorsky) system working and put it in production, starting absolutely from scratch with no prior knowledge, and in the very short time available, was a truly remarkable performance. The development of the (by now Westland) flight control system has proceeded to a stage of extreme complication in the Wessex Mk.3. The Wessex Mk.1 development programme rounded off some fifteen years of effort to consolidate our understanding of the problems of airworthiness and reliability in complex mechanisms.

This work has yielded a great deal of valuable information and a relatively clear insight into the means of achieving the extremely high standards now accepted as necessary for future aircraft. The lessons learned in this period have been the subject of many papers from the internal Stress Office and Type Test Engineering department, but some aspects were reported in my Cierva Memorial lecture of 1963 and in Brochure B.330 of January 1965 prepared for discussion by the S.B.A.C. Standing Committee on Reliability.

Up to the time of the mergers, Westland built helicopters to Sikorsky designs partly because initially they did not have adequate staff or facilities to do anything else, in view of the Wyvern commitment, but also and mainly because the production of helicopters for the Armed Services could best be carried out in this way since the Service requirements in effect described already existing American aircraft.

Nevertheless, from the outset it was the hope of the technical staff employed on helicopters at Westland that we would proceed as soon as possible to our own designs and there is no doubt that by the time the Company finally dropped fixed-wing aircraft, it did in fact have adequate staff and facilities for this purpose had original Westland designs been required.

Throughout this period, in spite of great pressure to meet production commitments, project investigations were undertaken as in any other aircraft company. This may be briefly summarised as follows.

From the beginning it was evident that the carrying capacity of the Dragonfly was limited as much by centre of gravity. problems as by power. One of the earliest studies was the provision of an additional cabin for two persons in the area of the baggage compartment plus the provision of two additional seats forward in the main cabin (i.e. a total of seven persons plus the pilot) and a mock-up of this arrangement was built. Later on, a number of alternative improvements to the Dragonfly were summarised in Brochure B.148 (June 1954). After a long delay a selection was made from these possibilities, resulting in the design of the Widgeon, an exercise which was invaluable in cementing a good relationship between the newly amalgamated fixed wing and helicopter design staffs.

This involved the introduction of the Whirlwind rotor head, upper gearbox and power controls, with the provision of an entirely new five-seat cabin with good provision for two stretchers and for carriage of freight. The control system of this aircraft was also greatly improved. Due to the initial delay, the Widgeon unfortunately appeared on the market at the same time as the French Alouette and was therefore never sold in large numbers, although it remains one of the most pleasant of this early generation of helicopters.

In 1953 an experimental four-bladed rotor was installed on a Dragonfly. The trials of this aircraft, and the associated studies, yielded valuable insights of significance for the future. Among other things, the possible uses of a second-harmonic feathering control were examined, and drawings were prepared for an experimental installation, though the trials were terminated before this could be carried out. The test results confirmed that stalling of the retreating blade of a rotorcraft does not necessarily limit forward speed.

The tests were conducted well beyond the onset of stalling and threw much valuable light on the distribution of lift over the rotor at high tip speed ratios, and on the significance of the higher harmonics of flapping and varying numbers of blades with respect to the causes, and possible cure, of helicopter vibration. These studies and test results were reported in my 1957 lecture to the Helicopter Association.

In 1954 Westland became interested in the possibility of building the Sikorsky S-56 under licence and a number of studies were done of the manner in which this aircraft might be re-engined using British turbines. One such study was outlined in Brochure B.149 (June 1954) showing the installation of Eland engines on the ends of the S-56 stub wing.

After a great deal of very forceful internal argument, it was finally accepted that the sensible thing to do was to keep to our own original proposals for mounting rear driving turbines ahead of the rotor above the cabin roof and this yielded the extremely promising study of Brochure B.158 (July 1955), which described the Westminster. When this brochure and its associated drawings were seen by Michael Gluhareff during a visit he was greatly impressed and it is probable that this was instrumental in establishing the design trend adopted by Sikorsky in many of their subsequent helicopters.

When Westland decided to proceed with the Westminster it was obvious that this very large development would have to be carried out with an absolute minimum of staff and resources. Our by that time considerable experience of the need for test rigs in the development of transmissions, engine installations and controls led us to propose a flying test rig on which all development running might be carried out and which would at the same time provide an opportunity for development of the cockpit and of the general handling properties of the aircraft.

The first Westminster flying test rig was built with a heavy airframe capable of carrying lead weights to simulate the full all-up weight of the Westminster and it was provided with a single tie-down point for development Type Testing. The fact that the aircraft had twin engines would have enabled the novel Westland part of the transmission design to be subjected to fatigue testing during tie-down running.

As in the case of the Widgeon, considerable departures were made from Sikorsky control design practice to provide more favourable control gearing, plus suitable feel, and the Westminster, which had automatic rotor speed governing, was reported to be one of the most pleasant helicopters ever built, from the pilot's point of view.

Unfortunately, the provision of a central tie-down point was used to persuade people outside the company that the openwork flying test rig had been designed as a crane, for which purpose it was in fact not very well suited, particularly in view of the deliberately high weight of the airframe. Westland private effort and expenditure on the Westminster raised objections at a high level in the Navy and the company was reprimanded for allegedly not proceeding as fast as possible with the Wessex. This allegation was quite untrue, and in fact the Wessex was flown well ahead of schedule. Nevertheless, Service opposition and a general lack of outside interest in the project led to its being abandoned.

Just before it was abandoned, Mr Hollis Williams thought there might be a chance of selling a few Westminsters with a lightened version of the openwork airframe and this, with other refinements, was built into the second prototype. In April 1958 the detailed specification of a monocoque airline version had been presented to the IATA Committee (Brochures International Air Transport Association 1 & 2), and design work was started on the monocoque airframe by Saunders-Roe at Cowes soon after that Company had merged with Westland in 1959. To supplement wind tunnel estimates of speed and stability, a streamlined fairing (in Terylene fabric with a special dope to withstand the E.E.L.6. lubricant used for the transmission) was added to the original prototype, which flew with a very low vibration level at 135 knots with a six-bladed rotor.

The Westminster as submitted to IATA was based on two Elands but the power of these engines was well below that originally promised by 'Napier' and the addition of a Gnome as a third engine cum A.P.U. was also envisaged. Over long stage lengths the Westminster was compared unfavourably with the Rotodyne and Type 194, and work on it was finally stopped after the mergers in 1960.

16 Here be Giant Killers

Jack Sweet

This anthology is primarily concerned with aviation as the underlying reason why Yeovil can no longer claim to be 'The Quiet Country Town' it was at the turn of the century. There was, however, one period of activity when the noise was generated by a group whose interest was far removed from technology.

In 1948/49, Yeovil Town Football Club entered the annual FA Cup competition. The team remained undefeated for five rounds, beating some of the powerful and wealthy clubs in the process; in doing so they earned the title 'Giant Killers'. The following items are rich with the flavour of the times, from the reports by Jack Sweet in the local newspaper the Western Gazette.

Around this time, Westland was about to deliver the first Yeovil-built Dragonfly helicopters.

In 1948 the people of Britain were recovering from five years of total war; industry was struggling to modernise and adapt to peacetime markets, and in everyday life, austerity and rationing was the norm and the demobilised forces were flooding the job market.

When Yeovil Town FC entered the FA Cup competition there was little expectation that they would last long. They won the first two matches, playing against teams of their own size, but in the third round they came up against the big boys; it was not until they played Manchester United in the fifth round that they left the competition with a nationwide reputation as 'Giant Killers'.

It was the stuff that dreams are made of.

YEOVIL *v* BURY 1949

The Yeovil streets were deserted when the bells of St John's rang in 1949 and in The Boro' only two young men welcomed in the New Year. However, the relative peace of the New Year was the calm before the town went football mad! On Saturday 8 January 1949 Yeovil, the only non-league team in the FA Cup third round, would take on 2nd Division Bury at the Huish ground.

A record crowd was expected and during the week 'three public spirited veteran supporters', glove manufacturer Edwin 'Tink' Robbins, Supporters Club Chairman 68 years old Ted Perrott, and retired brewery worker Ted Cooper, 71, laid dozens of railway sleepers and shovelled tons of earth to provide an extension for several hundred extra spectators on the Jubilee terrace. Hotels and guesthouses were full of national sports reporters and photographers, and camera teams from *Gaumont British News* were in town. Everything was ready for the big day: shops would shut, and businesses close and the pubs had obtained special licences to open for two hours on the Saturday afternoon 'to give supporters an opportunity for celebrating'. (Remember, this is 1949!)

They came from all across the West Country, in special trains, coaches, cars and on foot, filling the streets, and were queuing outside the ground four hours before the 2 o'clock kick-off. The crowd of 13,500 ticket holders packed into every inch of the stand and terraces; others perched on buildings, advertisement hoardings and in trees overlooking the ground. In the stand was staunch supporter 86-year-old Mrs Minnie Gilham from West Coker who came in to every home game and who, in the words of the *Western Gazette*'s reporter, had 'a surprising knowledge of the game and who was fully aware of the financial difficulties besetting small non-league clubs' – 'Win or lose I'll still continue to organise my whist drives in the village for Yeovil FC,' she declared. Good luck messages were received from many of Yeovil's partners in the Southern League and from supporters in all parts of the country.

To a roar of approval, the Yeovil team, led by its 10-year-old mascot, Rex Rainey, ran onto the pitch and what happened next is football history. Player manager Alec Stock's non-leaguers scored after seven minutes and never looked back, defeating Bury 3-1 – Yeovil's goals came from Jackie Hargreaves, Ray Wright and Bobby Hamilton.

At the final whistle, the crowd could contain themselves no longer and pouring onto the pitch, carried the Yeovil team shoulder high to the dressing rooms. The *Western Gazette* reported that 'Ninety thrilling minutes put an end to any financial qualms the Club might have had. Their share of the gate, which amounted to nearly £700, doubled the existing bank balance. Three months ago the club feared an overdraft. Gross receipts were £1,565.'

The result dropped the bookies' odds on Yeovil winning the FA Cup from 5,000–1 against to 500–1 against.

Speaking after the game, Bury's manager, Norman Bullock, told 'R.G.K.' of the *Gazette* that 'Yeovil were easily the better side and thoroughly deserved to go into the next round. Their standard of play was far better than he had expected, and they backed it up by lots of confidence and great team spirit.' When I asked him if the sloping pitch had played any part in Bury's downfall, Mr Bullock, the great sportsman that he is, replied: 'I should be the last person to suggest that this had anything to do with Yeovil's success. They played the right type of football and deservedly won on their merit. I wish them the best of luck in the next round.'

Four supporters from Taunton wrote to the *Western Gazette*'s Sports Editor expressing appreciation of the kindly co-operation of the residents of Queen Street whose back gardens adjoined one of the terraces. The Tauntonians had only a slender chance of seeing the game from the top of the packed terrace and 'asked two housewives over the garden wall if they could lend a stool. A chair and a stool were immediately forthcoming – excellent "platform" accommodation. The Good Samaritans resolutely declined any security for their property, and also declined a token of appreciation when it was returned.'

The Yeovil 'Giant Killers' were on their way to the fourth round of the FA Cup and next in their sights would be the 'mighty Sunderland'.

SUNDERLAND DEFEATED

'YEOVIL ASTONISH FOOTBALL WORLD' – cried the *Western Gazette* on 4 February 1949 and went on to tell how – 'Jubilant scenes reminiscent of VE Day followed Saturday's sensational Fourth Round FA Cup-tie by Yeovil Town's £100-a-week team of part-time professionals over Sunderland, a club which has never been out of the First Division and whose players cost over £60,000 in transfer fees. The town went wild with excitement and people who thronged the streets demonstrated their delight, forgetting their accustomed southern reserve. The celebrations were by no means confined to the town for wherever Somerset folk gathered the sole topic of conversation was Yeovil's success. There was, for instance, a terrific cheer when on the stage of the Pavilion Theatre at Bournemouth came a member of the cast wearing a huge green and white rosette, who laughingly commentated: "Roses are red and violets are blue, Sunderland one, Yeovil two."'

The Cup fever which had gripped Yeovil during the weeks leading up to the match on 29 January had resulted in an overwhelming demand for tickets even though the price of a seat in the stand had gone up to 10s 6d, and the enclosure to 7s 6d.; however, the ground tickets were held at 2s. But with no concessions to Supporters Club members or schoolboys, everyone wanted a ticket and in the words of the Yeovil Club Secretary – '35,000 people want to obtain admission to a ground which is limited to 15,000.' On 21 January, the *Western Gazette* reported that – 'Extraordinary scenes were witnessed at the ground on Tuesday when applicants for a limited number of ground tickets began queuing in the morning. First there was Mrs Beatrice Beacham, of 59 Garden City, Langport, who arriving at 11 a.m., waited eight hours to obtain a ticket for her 18-year-old son who plays for the Langport team. Hundreds, who waited throughout the afternoon, including elderly women and children, were served with tea by women members of the Supporters Club. Trouble brewed in the early evening when factory workers swarmed into the ground from all directions, and people who had been waiting in the queue for several hours found themselves in a milling and jostling crowd of 2,000 with no hope of obtaining tickets. There were angry scenes and cat-calls as a section of the crowd made a rush for the ticket office and police reinforcements had to be sent to the ground. When the police and Club officials were finding difficulty in holding the angry and disappointed crowd in check, Supt. F.B. Hanham made a timely intervention and appealed to them to go home quietly. 'I am disgusted and ashamed,' he said. 'I have seen occurrences like this in other towns but I never thought it could happen at Yeovil.' The Superintendent promised some hope for disappointed supporters when he said: 'If the ground capacity should be extended and more tickets are printed I will do what I can to help everyone to get a square deal.' The *Western Gazette* went on to refer to trouble outside a couple of evening newspaper offices when their allocation of tickets was sold out within twenty minutes.

However, the problems of the tickets had evaporated by the big day as the crowd began to form outside the ground at 8 o'clock and by the time the gates opened at noon, the queue stretched, six deep, for nearly half a mile along Huish, through Clarence Street and into The Park. Fog delayed many of the 1,000 or so Sunderland supporters, who travelled the 400 miles from County Durham to Yeovil by road and rail, until after the kick off. A coach party from a Sunderland working men's club who found themselves without accommodation following a booking mix up were rescued by Yeovil Labour Club whose members found overnight rooms for the visitors.

Over 17,000 ticket holders were finally packed into the Huish ground, whilst the ticketless watched from the windows and roofs of adjoining houses, the brewery buildings in Clarence Street or listened to the BBC commentary relayed from police car radios.

History tells us that Yeovil won but unless you were there, words cannot convey the atmosphere – I was near the goal at the Clarence Street end and it was something never to be forgotten. Resplendent in their new strip of green and white presented by the ladies' section of the Supporters Club and with the town's coat of arms on their shirts, the Yeovil team ran onto the pitch to a deafening roar from the crowd and after tearing into Sunderland for twenty-six minutes, player manager Alec Stock placed the ball in the back of the visitor's net – Yeovil 1 Sunderland 0. Fifteen minutes into the second half Sunderland equalised but inspired defending and constant attacking Yeovil forwards kept the score level and the game went into extra time. By now the atmosphere was electric and the emotion released fourteen minutes later when Yeovil's Eric Bryant scored could almost be seen. Alec Stock's team held on for the remaining fifteen minutes and at the final whistle Yeovil was in the fifth round of the FA Cup.

In the Club's boardroom after the match, Sunderland's Chairman, Colonel 'Joe' Prior, raised his glass to his hosts and said, 'You have won the game deservedly, yours are a grand lot of lads and their splendid team spirit won them the match. If in the next round you are again drawn at home and you play as you did today you will go a long way in the Cup. A lot has been said about your ground but I like it. In all my years of football I have never experienced such a warm welcome as I have had at Yeovil and although we have lost – it will be a shock to the folk back home – it has been well worth it to find such friendship and hospitality. My only regret is that we were unable to force a draw and repay your kindness at Roker Park.'

Yeovil's record-breaking Cup run was not over and next on the list was Manchester United.

YEOVIL AT MANCHESTER

Yeovil's win against the 'mighty Sunderland' and entry into the fifth round of the FA Cup brought congratulations at the rate of several hundred a day from across the country, from West Country emigrants in Australia, South Africa and Canada, supporters in Sweden, Switzerland and Germany and from service personnel in garrisons around the world. The Mayor, Alderman Ben Dening, received a midnight telephone call from the News Editor of the *Ontario Star* telling him how his readers had been thrilled by Yeovil's success and wanting to know all about the town and its winning team.

Yeovil was drawn to play the winners of the replay between Bradford and Manchester United and on 4 February the waiting was over – it would be the Cup holders and 7–2 favourites Manchester United away at Maine Road on 12 February. Yeovil's Chairman, Bert Smith, was delighted with the result commenting that 'It is the best draw we could have wished for and we are assured of the biggest gate of at least 80,000.'

Cup-tie fever raged through the town with many factories and businesses deciding to make the trip to Manchester as their annual outing and one glove factory booked a special train for its 600 employees. Special trains were laid on by British Rail with the Manchester return fare at 37s 6d (£1.85) and dozens of coaches were hired to make the 250 mile journey.

'R.G.K.' of the *Western Gazette*, who was travelling with the team, described their departure: 'Engine whistles shrieked and detonators exploded on the line as the gaily bedecked train in green and white pulled out from Pen Mill Station yesterday (Thursday) morning taking Yeovil Town's team of part-time professional footballers to meet the holders Manchester United at Maine Road tomorrow (Saturday) in the 5th Round of the FA Cup.

'Will Yeovil's team of players drawn from factory, workshop and office make modern soccer history, by being the first non-league club to reach the 6th Round of the competition? This was the question uppermost in the minds of the crowd who gave them a resounding send-off. There were cheers, too, from the many early morning workers, as they arrived at the station to catch their buses to local factories.

'Before the team left, a portable wireless was presented by Mr J. Hart, a gift which Mr Hart promised the Chairman if the team beat Sunderland in the last round of the Cup.

'At the last minute several players rushed from the train to fetch the crate of eggs and sherry, the match-winning tonic, which had somehow been overlooked.

'News of the team's departure spread all along the line and I saw groups of people lining wayside stations where "Good Luck" slogans appeared overnight.'

The supporters, including the Mayor, left for the north by road and rail in what was described as the biggest exodus the town had ever known and over 3,000 fans on six special trains set off late Friday for the overnight journey to Manchester.

Although the February sky was grey and cold, the welcome the Yeovil team and it supporters received in Manchester could not have been warmer. At Lewis's Market Street Department Store, with seating for 2,000, Yeovil supporters were offered special breakfasts, lunches and teas to keep out the cold and hotels made available wash and brush-up facilities for the fans after their long overnight journey.

From the time the Yeovil team arrived in the city they were feted and 'R.G.K.' recounted how they were 'Idolised by a Cup-frenzied populace. Besieged by admirers and autograph hunters in the streets, stores and in theatres and cinemas they many times had to seek police aid.' Hundreds of messages of support reached the team in their hotel, including one from Gloversville in the USA. 'R.G.K.' could hardly contain himself as he reported that 'Six thousand West Country fans brought colour and noise to a drab Manchester on Saturday morning. With rattles, bells, motor horns and a drum, they told the city that theirs was no small-town team. They even brought a special Yeovil-made glove in green and white with an 18-inch span and two and a half feet long. Outrivalled only by Wembley were the amazing scenes at Maine Road. All gates were closed 20 minutes before the kick-off, when it was estimated that there were 80,000 in the ground (the gate was 81,565). Thousands were locked out.

One hour before the match was due to commence many of the gates on the popular side were closed. So dense was the crowd inside that several hundred youngsters were passed over the heads of waiting onlookers and were allowed to sit inside the wall behind the touch line. Thousands of soccer fans had queued in crowded Manchester Piccadilly for 'buses which moved off at the rate of one every 30 seconds'.

As for the match, Yeovil's part timers had no real hope against the Cup holders with six internationals on the field playing before their home crowd, and the defeat of 8–0 was not unexpected. However, Yeovil fought gallantly and United's manager, the great Matt Busby, said that Alec Stock's team had 'Played hard and never gave up trying – their display was a credit to non-league clubs.' Manchester's Vice-Chairman, Harold Hardman, praised the team in no uncertain terms: 'It has been the most sporting game we have seen at Maine Road this season. Yeovil have left a lasting impression.'

Thus Yeovil's dreams of Cup glory ended but the team and its supporters could look back on an exciting few weeks in the drab winter of 1949 and a place in football legend.

During the same period, the first WS-51 Dragonfly helicopters were nearing completion at the Westland factory, and the changeover to helicopters was under way.

4 January 2015. History repeats itself.

Serendipity is a wonderful thing. No sooner had the centenary year commenced than Yeovil Town FC found themselves having to confront Manchester United yet again as an FA cup opponent.

The match engendered considerable excitement and memories of 1949, and perhaps some apprehension. But as it turned out there was nothing to fear; the Yeovil team held their formidable opponents to a goalless draw until well into the second half.

The final score was a 2-0 win for Manchester and the winning team joined in a standing ovation for the Yeovil players. Maybe next year: Fee, Fo, Fi, Fum ...

17 Wyvern

Harald Penrose

The Wyvern was a powerful propeller-driven Naval Strike Fighter, designed and built at Yeovil between 1945 and 1956. There were a number of incidents, mainly concerning the variable-pitch Contra rotating propeller mechanism which resulted in a very poor safety record. Harald Penrose famously stated: 'Very nearly a very good aircraft.'

It did enter service and saw action at Suez, it performed well and was highly thought of by those who flew it.

In his book No Echo in the Sky *Harald Penrose described some of his experiences.*

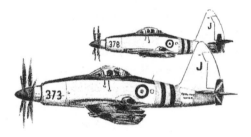

Like a procession of great cumulus clouds, painted with sunlight and shadows, year after year had sailed into the past. Looking back it seemed a far cry to the day when flying first enthralled me with wings of canvas stretched tight with dope upon a wooden frame of spindled spars and latticed ribs, and propelled by a stuttering rotary engine.

Step by step, aeroplanes had become more mechanically purposeful and complicated. The bird-like purity of control of machines with small inertia had gone, and we accepted without further thought the ponderous flight of heavily laden wings drawn by fantastic power at speeds which annihilated time and distance.

The Wyvern, a strike fighter, which I tested through difficult years between its initial flight in 1949 and introduction to squadrons in 1953, was the three hundred and ninetieth type I had flown. It had huge, turbine-driven, contra-rotating double propellers which gave a misleading air of anachronism among the rapier-pointed jets. With wing area little greater than my light aeroplane of old, it was heavier than the twin-engined transports which only five years earlier had carried detachments of fully armed parachute troops to an invasion designed to be the end of war. Yet in the succeeding days of peace man lived more uneasily than ever before, filled with foreboding.

So my task remained the same as in the beginning: developing and making safe for other pilots ever newer forms of airborne death; and finding in that strange pursuit fulfilment of the mind's most eager striving, because it let me see the world, the universe, and men in their most profound relationship – and in so doing let me find myself.

This time there were no vast heights to scale. The measure of progress was that the Wyvern could lift four times the weight twice as high as a similar aeroplane of twenty years before. Its speed did not approach that of the latest jet-reaction fighters which could already escape the sound of their passing, but it flew faster than the swiftest fighter of the 1939–45 war, and nearly five times the speed of the little Widgeon monoplane of those long ago days in the dawning age of flight.

From the beginning when the engine of the Mark I prototype stopped suddenly as a result of ignition failure 20,000 feet above a low layer of stratus cloud, it sharpened our wits. The cause of that first forced landing was comparatively unimportant, but, as always with the development flying of the Wyvern, it was the effect which was grave. Although the all-up weight corresponded to that of a Dakota, the wing-loading, more than 60lb per square foot, was nearly three times as heavy. Consequently, when the engine cut, the Wyvern dropped, more like a brick than an aeroplane, in a fast, steep dive because it became impossible to feather the propeller; and the enormous drag created by the large, flat, paddle-shaped blades in original use, made it very difficult to flatten out for landing. On that occasion I hurtled through the cloud base at 3,000 feet to find the disused aerodrome of Warmwell luckily within reach. Miraculously, the machine landed safely between hidden concrete blocks that had been scattered over the entire overgrown area to dissuade German airborne invaders.

The first eventful circuit of the later prototype powered by the gas-turbine replacing the Rolls-Royce piston engine, was the briefest initial flight I have ever made. It lasted barely three minutes. At that moment of becoming airborne, the cabin filled with dense, acrid smoke. I had to turn on full oxygen to breathe, and landed unable to see the instruments and convinced the machine was on fire.

Yet there was no real cause for anxiety. The fumes had escaped from a hydraulic leak pouring on to the hot case covering the incandescent gases behind the combustion chamber.

The main problem of the Wyvern's long and laborious development arose, however, from the installation of the turbo-prop power unit. Turbine thrust was adjusted by control of the propeller pitch which could be changed as quickly as the pilot moved the throttle, enabling thrust to be cut sharply for landing on an aircraft carrier. Whilst satisfying the deck landing requirements, the rapid pitch change of the propeller was, at high speeds, inclined to release the energy stored in the rotating parts of the engine, and bring about violent surges in the thrust of the turbine.

In proving the solution, a colleague and I did a long series of dives to see if the engine/propeller speed control was liable to run away and cause serious damage. With each pull-out subjecting us to 3G or 4G, we were very tired by the time we had accomplished a thousand dives; but the investigation established the reliability of the control unit and led the way to endorsive tests by Naval test pilots.

Before this there came a particular moment in the sequence of testing when, my job complete, I had prolonged the flight to throw circle after circle in the clear sky of late summer afternoon, loath to forsake the high view of Wessex drowsing in sunlight. Presently I throttled the turbine, and the tandem propellers on their single shaft hummed in a long, straight glide from three miles high to the home aerodrome.

At 800 feet I opened the engine to a livelier tune, and started a gentle turn to bring the aeroplane round for the approach circuit. With no imminent danger, disaster struck wildly, flinging the machine into a violent sideways swirl. The sky spun round, no longer over my head, but under my feet. Ten times swifter than normal thought, subconscious animal instinct had swept the control column across the cockpit in the opposite direction to the wild sideways spin. The ailerons were ominously weightless, giving no perceptible response; yet the rotation slowed and I was left hanging inverted in the straps, diving upside down at rows of neat red houses set with the distortion of a dream above my head.

I could see no escape. The machine was uncontrollable and those wedge-shaped roofs were already barely 500 feet away. The seconds were luminous and still. A fraction longer of living and then walls would crash asunder as the aeroplane shattered into fragments under a pall of flame and oily smoke. From far away I watched my end dispassionately.

Yet swiftly, in the fleeting instant between life and death, the ponderous machine was doing strange and unexpected things. The upward rush of chimney pots and roofs was checked. My inherent aerobatic training, practised for pleasure these many years, had pushed the control column diagonally forward into the far corner of the cockpit, and kicked maximum rudder hard across in the same direction. Shuddering, the inverted nose lifted until the propeller fanned against the sky. Screwed round by the rudder, the massive aeroplane violently flick-rolled its ten tons. The houses dropped and dwindled as the wings swirled right way up through normal lateral level, and wobbled left and right on the edge of stalling. Then the machine regained balance and climbed steadily to the safety of higher skies.

Moving my head with cautious deliberation, as though it might disturb the machine's precarious equilibrium, I looked through the side windows. Both ailerons were deflected to their maximum upward angle, locked hard against their stops. One must have broken free from the controlling mechanism, and been flung full up by the press of air upon the aerodynamic balance in front of its hinge. The opposite aileron was still serviceable, and only then did I see that it was my own hand which held it firmly applied to counteract the violent cartwheeling effect of the other wing. Maybe five seconds had elapsed from start to finish of that wild gyration – five swift seconds separating unsuspecting sunlit peace from restored and grateful sunlight.

Few had escaped from so close a call as this. Up ... up ... gently ... steadily ... I willed her towards higher skies, still holding the stick unnaturally across the cockpit to balance the live aileron against the broken. Up and up we laboured towards the life-giving sun, where height spells safety for a parachute descent should the machine prove uncontrollable when I tried to turn and had to bank a wing once more. The fair and familiar landscape was serene in the sunshine as my gaze swept from horizon to horizon. I was a mote in those skies, floating without volition on the tide of time which would be flowing long after the last man had gone to dust.

With infinite caution I began to turn, and knew at once that a landing was within little more than normal limits of judgement. In a five-mile circuit, barely banking lest we rolled over, I edged the Wyvern round into the approach. I felt a sense of unreality, and insecurity as the machine carried me towards the aerodrome. Each second passed with a strange mental clarity. Each threatened that with the next the Wyvern must lurch violently, roll wing down, and drop uncontrollably as it had done three minutes earlier. But cold logic insisted that the flight was safe, that the upturned aileron gave lateral equilibrium far greater than the machine's normal stability. Had not the same thing happened to me years ago when the Whirlwind aileron control burned through?

Nevertheless, part of me, crouching, keyed up, waited for the wing to drop; waited for the rapidly approaching moment when the glide would bring the machine below the height at which the cartridge ejector seat offered a last reasonable chance of parachute escape. I pressed the transmitter switch and gave my call sign. 'Judwin, priority landing. Finals from the west.'

'Judwin, finals,' confirmed a dispassionate voice. But if the voice sounded unfeelingly disinterested, the apparent lack of concern was belied by the sudden movement of fire tender and ambulance towards the point where I should touch down.

The undercarriage locked into position with its usual thump, and without, to my relief, any disturbance of trim sometimes produced by lack of phase in the movements of each leg. I had plenty of height in hand, and opened the flaps gently, notch by notch, to maximum lift. The right wing sank a fraction under the changed airflow. No aileron could be applied to check the motion. The wing rose level, stabilised by the negative tip angle of the upturned ailerons. Everything in order: the engine running fast: the aerodrome widening from a finger strip to a broad, green path. The red of the fire tender stood out beyond the trees, its crew looking up at the heavy monoplane. The boundary hedge flashed past, and the tyres touched the turf at 100mph.

I cut the engine. The turbine slowed with a sharp indrawn breath, followed by the diminishing whisper of the changing pitch of the propeller. My life on earth had begun anew.

Seven times that aeroplane brought me to grave hazard. From the eighth I escaped by the toss of a coin, which decided that Peter Garner, my close friend and assistant chief test pilot, would fly for some air-to-air photography of the Wyvern. 'I'd like to see my name in the papers for once instead of yours,' he joked.

A final close-up completed the air photography session. Peter gave a friendly wave of farewell, and turned for base. Within seconds the propeller bearing failed. He tried to make a forced landing in a very small field, but was unable to flare off the glide. The Wyvern hit the ground with undercarriage up and burst into flames.

Peter and Jimmy, Michael and Ted – yes, and all the others who had died untimely in the preceding years both of peace and war. With what light-hearted defiance they flung their brief days against the weighted scales of time, ventured the unattained, achieved their heart's desire, and in the moment of seeming triumph surrendered the flame of life.

These were the terms of the gamble: not an eye for an eye and a tooth for a tooth, but their own irreplaceable lives wagered against the spirit's aspiration – and always in the background was the muffled toll of bells. Though man is born to trouble as the sparks fly upward, youth does not live with introspective premonition in the sunshine of his life. The consciousness of peril becomes sublimated in other things, for it seems so safe high in the air with the world remote, and its people and occasions almost forgotten.

In any exploration of the boundaries of knowledge, fate will stab with the same sudden blindness as in everyday normal life. If in all things there are moments when luck alone can bring one through, a pilot's practised judgement has been conditioned by difficult circumstances to be prepared for the abnormal. So the most hazardous incidents of prototype flying leave no greater impression than the many fleeting moments of stress and difficulty encountered during the routine operation of fully developed production aeroplanes. Controls fail, structures break, stability vanishes, loads increase beyond the power of arms and feet, engines catch fire, propellers race and break, jet turbines over-speed or lose their blades, and every prototype I have ever flown has had at least one engine failure resulting in a forced landing. Nevertheless, such things are quickly forgotten in the accepted daily risks that are inseparably part of the technique of flying.

Flight must always be made in such a manner that the unknown can be met in a way that leaves some avenue of escape. As a last resort there is the parachute: sometimes fate trembles on the finest thread.

If anything, danger enhanced, rather than detracted from, the peerless fascination of gazing from the heights at the loveliness of the earth: a fascination poignant in the knowledge that such beauty bloomed for every man with the transience of a summer flower.

Whatever befell, each flight remained for me a reincarnation. Always there was new discovery of old and familiar things. Some days would be remembered for ever, whilst others might slip into the limbo of forgotten love. Such small things make remembrance: a look, a touch, a sudden vision of perfection, or the darkness of despair. And some gained forgetfulness because they were only part of a mere sequence leading to the unexpected.

So it was with the strike fighter and the thousand flights I made with her in one variant or another during the course of her protracted trials. Despite difficulties of development greater than the customary share, the Wyvern gave hundredfold enthralment for every hazard. Day after day and many times each day, breathing oxygen automatically controlled, we would climb through the blue skies, until high enough to dive at maximum speed, often pulling out so heavily that iron bands tightened on the temples, our jaws sagged, and the skies darkened as black-out point was reached. Controls applied at extreme angles made the ten-ton fighter lurch and slither in fantastic angles and attitudes as forces and movements were measured to provide the data for long calculations by the technical staff, structural alterations of controls or stabilising surfaces, and a further succession of check flights.

So the development of the aeroplanes continued. Sometimes the imagined remedy made the problem worse, but it was only a temporary setback in the gradual elimination of faults and the evolution of responses which custom had standardised as safe.

From the warm stillness of the bubble-canopied cockpit I watched, in the pauses between each test, the endless permutations of sky and sea and land. Any place in England was within an hour's reach. In a few minutes of full throttle I could leave the landscape far below, reaching steeply upwards to rediscover the eternities of sun-filled space.

At other times I might linger at low altitudes, flaps extended, the turbine whirling with the quiet rumbling of low power, and the propellers spinning their strange shadow of a cross fixedly ahead.

Beneath the slow passage of my wings the pattern of mounds and scars on the downland once more told a moment's story: gleaming chalk cliffs revealed the epic of ancient waters; and granite bastions defied the menacing seas. By grace of flight England became mine for the possessing. For a few brief minutes I was no longer a pilot flying a creation of complex mechanism, but disembodied, sailing the heavens on angel's wings.

The months of developing the Wyvern mounted into years, until eventually they brought in the late hours of a calm summer afternoon a production machine for test. The haze which for some days had tinted the landscape with tired blue and drawn the horizon close had given way to crystal-clear visibility. On a faint drift of air two miles above the earth an armada of great cumulus slowly sailed. From 20,000 feet above them I could see hundreds of square miles of green and corn-coloured fields stretching into the distance, every line of their blue-green hedges sharp and distinct.

At far intervals in the stillness of the lower skies faint curtains of smoke delineated the shape of distant towns. Demarcations of coast etched the outlines of the lands north and south. On my right was the broad rift of the Bristol Channel, one shore visible from Pembroke far up the Severn into Gloucester. The other embraced Wessex, stretching past Exmoor to Bideford Bay which glittered like a mirror below the shadowed line of the Atlantic. Beyond my left shoulder spread the blue sequin sea of the Channel, its deckled coastline painted with brilliant detail all the way from Beachy Head westward to the dark loom of Start Point silhouetted above the deep blue of Falmouth Bay.

Time was pressing. Exceptional though the view might be today it must wait for some less hurried moment. It was my possession; and would always be waiting there no less enchanting whenever I needed to attain it. But in this hour I must be occupied with more urgent matters. I accepted the compromise that had been made so many times before. The readings of the rows of dials were noted on my pad.

Now for the dive. The hood-lock was checked, harness straps strained tighter; trimmers reset. After a quick scrutiny for other aircraft, and a last glance at the instrument panel, I depressed the long nose. The slipstream rose in a crescendo until the limiting speed was attained and held. I crouched in the cabin head bent to the instruments, senses tuned to the vibrations of the aeroplane, diving on the gyros blind to the outside world. The touch of the controls and the sound of the engine registered that all was well. At 7,000 feet I pulled steadily into level flight and slowed with throttled engine. I glanced outside for a visual check on my position, and I saw again, with a sense of benediction, the far beauty of the waiting landscape. But others too were waiting. I called the dispersal aerodrome and began the brief descent.

Five minutes later I taxied to the tarmac apron by the entrance to the hangar. Cocks were cut and electrics switched off. The engine gasped to a stop and all was silent. I cranked back the hood, and watched a ladder being dragged to the wing. The foreman clambered up: 'They want you to call at the administration office on your way home,' he reported. 'They said it's urgent.' I nodded absently and unpinned my safety harness and parachute. 'That elevator was much better,' I said. 'We'll do the aft loading tomorrow.'

Through the winding lanes and roads of a dreamy countryside the car carried me swiftly back to the offices. I took the photographic results to the technical section and turned to the administration block. It was not until I went up the stairs that I wondered what could be so urgent.

In kindly fashion they broke the news: 'There's another job we'd like you to tackle. We think it is time you gave up test flying. Twenty-five years is a longish spell.'

What were they telling me? Give up flying? Twenty-five years? It was long before that I had started to fly. With no warning was this the end? Why had there been no sign, no portent in the skies – only an urgent test that gave no time for the leisured enjoyment of flight?

The news was like the sudden catastrophe which in those years of flying had many times disrupted the oblivious quiet. But just as a sleeping awareness of danger had underlain my every flight, I had always known that one day there must come an end to this enchanting quest of the skies. Better suddenly like this than shirking from the last farewell, the final touch, and the emptiness as one turns away.

Yet it seemed impossible to say 'Good-bye'. Year after year the skies had been mine – the eternal skies, magically repainted from hour to hour with changing combinations of mist and cloud and light. So often in that vast blue emptiness I had sat absorbed and silent, enfolded in my thoughts and action, waiting without impatience for time to go. If now I could but gather it up again and fly through time once more: the space, the freedom, the happiness, the answer almost heard. 'We know it will be a wrench – but let's have your decision tomorrow,' they said.

In the calm evening I slowly walked home through the woods. No tree stirred. I walked without consciousness. No bird sang – for the time of their rapture was gone. I looked up. In the highest zenith a contrail grew across the cloudless blue – but there was no echo in the sky. Everything was silent. The trail travelled swiftly to the far horizon, the aeroplane unseen, leaving only the slowly expanding vapour path to tell of the quietness that in the infinities of outer space awaits the quenchless, questing spirit of man.

18 Rationalisation

David Gibbings

The viable helicopter emerged upon the aviation scene towards the end of the Second World War, and as the aircraft industry adapted to peacetime, so helicopters were adopted as part of their activity. By 1955 there were several companies with well-established rotorcraft groups and by 1960, the British aircraft industry had been transformed with the result that Westland emerged as the sole major helicopter company.

David Gibbings was working with the Fairey Aviation Company at the time.

In the years that followed the Second World War, the British Aircraft Industry regrouped to meet the challenge of peacetime. By the late 1950s there were about twenty aircraft manufacturers.

As time progressed it became apparent that the major problem was that each potential order resulted in the design and manufacture of at least two prototypes.

The result was that the whole procurement process was becoming inefficient and costly.

After vigorous debates in Parliament, a White Paper was produced, calling for the industry to regroup into larger, more efficient units, and it was further emphasised that future orders for military aircraft and civil machines required for government controlled airline companies would go to the organisations that followed the Government's wishes.

It should, however, be pointed out that the 'White Paper' contained some very odd assumptions, including a statement that 'The day of the manned fighter was over, and that future aerial warfare would be resolved with guided weapons!'

The 'White Paper' was recognised for the threat it was and during the two years that followed, the industry was thrown into turmoil as the companies vied with each other to join one or other of the reformed groups. Many famous names disappeared, such as de Havilland, Hawker, Avro, and Vickers, and the British Aircraft Industry changed forever.

When the dust had settled, the airframe industry had refined into two large organisations:

The British Aircraft Corporation:

Boulton Paul
Bristol
English Electric
Hunting-Percival
Supermarine
Vickers

The Hawker-Siddeley Group:

Armstrong-Whitworth
Avro
Blackburn
De-Havilland
Folland
Gloster
Hawker

There were a few companies that either resisted the change, or were not taken up by the big two.

Perhaps the most notable of these was Handley-Page. Led by its founder Sir Frederick Handley-Page, it became clear that there was no way that the Handley-Page Company was going to join up with anybody, other than as leader.

With production of the Victor bomber, Hermes and Herald airliners, the company was able to survive until 1970. Auster and Miles aircraft, joined together, and with support from Pressed Steel Ltd, continued as Beagle Aircraft Ltd, producing light aircraft from their Rearsby and Woodley factories, eventually joining Handley-Page as Handley-Page Reading Ltd.

Scottish Aviation continued to produce their Pioneer and Twin Pioneer Utility aircraft, and with the demise of Beagle and Handley-Page, took over the Jetstream, but eventually ceased trading in 1977.

Shorts were in a unique position, in that they were situated in Northern Ireland, an area the government were pledged to support. They continued with their own range of light airliners until 1980, when they were taken over by Bombardier of Canada.

The Helicopter Industry

It quickly became clear that the two major aircraft groups had no wish to become involved in rotorcraft. There were four companies whose primary business was with helicopters:

The Helicopter Division of the Bristol Aircraft Company

This was formed under the leadership of Raoul Hafner, who was himself one of the pioneers of the helicopter and autogiro. The company was producing Sycamore and Belvedere.

Neither of these machines were on order in sufficient quantities to ensure that Bristol could take the lead, and they were absorbed by Westland in 1960.

The Fairey Aviation Company

Fairey was technically very strong, with a range of diverse projects such as the Fairey Delta 2 and the Gannet AEW, but they were also fully engaged in the development of the Ultra-Light and Rotodyne helicopters. Apart from the 44 Gannet AEW aircraft, they were completely reliant upon development contracts financed by the government under a process known as 'Cost + 10 per cent', the rationalisation programme that was about to be put in place, and was intended to put a stop to this cosy arrangement. The result was that Fairey were also taken over by Westland in 1960.

Saunders-Roe

The Saunders-Roe Company was a long-established aircraft manufacturer that had entered their helicopter business when they acquired the Cierva Company in 1950. Saunders-Roe was taken over by Westland in 1958.

The Westland Aircraft Company

Westland made its decision to specialise in helicopters in 1947. In order to achieve this, they negotiated an agreement to build established Sikorsky helicopters under licence; this included the right to sell their helicopters worldwide. The agreement had been extended to include several Sikorsky designs, such that they had built and sold some 600 helicopters by 1960, and from this financially strong situation, they were able to take the lead in restructuring the helicopter business. The amalgamation of the four companies brought together a strong design group coupled with a well-tested manufacturing capability.

For the workforce involved, it was a disturbing period, and it took a long time for the old, long established loyalties to die, but once the new enlarged Westland Helicopters Limited emerged as Britain's sole helicopter company, the scene was set for unprecedented growth and prosperity.

The rationalisation was a defining moment for the British aerospace industry, and similar upheavals were taking place worldwide. It marked the beginning of globalisation.

19 Westland 1947–1968

John Fay

John Fay joined the Royal Navy as a pilot early in the war; he served in Europe, including on the arctic convoys and in the Pacific. Flying Swordfish Albacores and Grumman Avengers, he was one of the first RN pilots to be trained to fly the early Sikorsky helicopters, and played an active part in the introduction of helicopters into the Royal Navy. In 1947 he joined the BEA Experimental Helicopter Unit and subsequently joined Westland as a test pilot. John has played an active part in the development of helicopters in the UK, and in this article which he has written specifically for this book he offers a clear insight into the early days at Yeovil.

My introduction to Westland began in 1947 when the BEA Helicopter Unit was formed. The aircraft operated were three Sikorsky-built S-51s and two Bell 47-Bs. The latter had open cockpits, but modifications were done later to give them enclosed cockpits, making them much more popular with the pilots. The initial venue as an operational base was Westland Aircraft Ltd, as it was thought that firm could be of assistance in many ways. Despite the fact that the BEA S-51s that the unit possessed were American-built by Sikorsky, Westland always referred to them as Westland-built, either because they were embarrassed that we were using American aircraft, or as an advertisement for their own British-built aircraft. These were slowly beginning to come off the line at the time.

In those days Westland was considerably smaller than it is today. The office space was miniscule compared with the large blocks we have now. Instead of several managers there was just one Commercial Manager who appeared to do everything. The gentleman there at that time, and later, was a Mr Williams, who later achieved fame by being bonked on the conk by Alan Bristow, who was then the only helicopter test pilot. Had Alan not been fired he would undoubtedly have become Chief Test Pilot; as it was he went off and became a multi-millionaire instead. The airfield itself was grazed by sheep, but this was only possible after flying was finished for the day when enormous gates would be shut and the sheep could be released into the field. The gates would prevent the sheep from wandering through the works.

Mr Oliver FitzWilliams, usually known as 'Fitz', was the Chief Engineer in 1947 and he was still there five years later when I joined Westland. He had a great sense of humour and a great way of explaining complicated things in a simple way. He was a great help to me. He later became Research Director. There was also a rather eccentric man called Leslie Lansdowne who used to wander into the pilots' office and tell us about the weather. He was a good friendly sort. I understood his line of work was to check items in manufacture that did not quite meet the correct specifications. I gave a flight to Eric Mensforth (later Sir Eric Mensforth) in a Bell 47-B. Later on as a member of Westland I met him many times and flew him quite often.

The BEA Helicopter Unit had its offices in the Bellman hangar, which were actually built while the personnel were starting operations. These consisted mainly of dummy mail runs around Somerset and Dorset and including places such as Bournemouth and Poole. Strangely, I was to occupy those same offices when I ran the pilot training school some five years later. The dummy mail operations were made primarily to enable the Post Office to study the economics of using helicopters to carry mail for them. I believe that the PO partly, or perhaps totally, financed the venture as a consequence. Later on, a smaller mail run using the Bells was started and was called the Clover Leaf. The routes were entirely local and we never went more than about 30 miles on this run.

The BEA Helicopter Unit stayed with Westland until April 1948 when it moved to a new base in Peterborough. The five aircraft flew in formation all the way. This location was chosen because of the flatness of the land in Norfolk and Suffolk to the east, making the flying safer for the next stage of the operations, which was to carry real mail around the countryside by day and night. The night service ran between Peterborough and Norwich and many were the times that practically the whole flight was carried out in blind flying conditions.

During the next few years I was twice on loan to Westland to carry out some urgent flying training. During the second occasion some wit coined a couplet: 'Captain Fay – is here to stay.' And stay I did – after a lapse of a few months.

Ted Wheeldon was Managing Director when I arrived in 1952. He was a very friendly down-to-earth approachable man and he called us by our first names. David Collins (later Sir David Collins) was Works Manager, and many were the phone calls I had to make to him when I was trying to run the flying school. Apart from the Chief Test Pilot, the Technical Director was Mr Hollis Williams, who was in charge of flying and matters pertaining. At one time I gave him a few hours' dual instruction in a helicopter (he was an ex-fixed-wing pilot), but he never had time to have a full course.

When I joined Westland we had Harald Penrose as Chief Pilot. He had been flying for so long that it was said that he had been on the same pilot's course as Pontius. There were only two other pilots, Roy Bradley and Derrick Colvin. Harald did not fly helicopters as he did not like them. His main complaint was that to go faster in a fixed-wing aircraft one pushed a lever forward with your left hand. If you did this in a helicopter you merely went down. This was in the day when the controls were manually operated – and very heavy they were too – so that the collective-pitch lever was very long to lessen the force needed to move it, so at the top of its arc the pilot was moving it forward or backwards. Nowadays, with power-operated controls, the collective-pitch lever needs to be operated through only an inch or two in an up and down movement to achieve the same result – a much more sensitive control, in fact. Servo controls were first tried out in the Dragonfly while I was in BEA and I remember travelling to Westland to try them out and give them my opinion.

I joined Westland in 1952 as a test pilot and instructor. It was the instructing that kept me busy most of my early time there for there was much training to be done and few places where it could be carried out or, indeed, experienced pilots who could do the job. If people were going to buy helicopters they must have pilots to fly them, and that is where the school was most important. The main source of pilots to be trained was from the RAF and I was fortunate to have many of them who had been through the Central Flying School so they were able to pass on some of their wisdom and, of course, they were excellent students who picked up helicopter flying fairly easily. I also trained pilots from France, Switzerland, Norway, Sweden, Italy, Mexico, Iraq, Iran, Jordan, Kuwait, Brazil, Yugoslavia, Egypt and Japan.

The language problem often proved difficult and it is amusing to note that the Italians were trained using the Italian language! I didn't speak it, but I learnt various phrases on the ground and used them in the air. Thus I would tell them to 'volo firmo', i.e. 'come to the hover,' or 'gira a sinistra' for 'turn left'. They much appreciated this and presented me with a watch when they left. My hardest task was with the Japanese, for their English was very limited. They were former kamikaze pilots and if I told people I trained kamikaze pilots they would look at me askance, wondering how I came to train enemy pilots. But, of course, these pilots were the lucky ones for the war ended before they had finished their training and they had never been called to sacrifice themselves for their country. I think their experience of fixed-wing flying was very limited and I had the greatest difficulty in getting them to solo standard. As regards the language problem, we had to sit together in the classroom while I said various things such as 'stick forward' and moved a walking stick forward in my hand while they would repeat my words until they understood them and the action required.

The Yugoslav pilots spoke reasonable English. I did manage to learn one word of Serbo-Croat, '*Peddy set-pet*', which meant 55. However, the aircraft were S-55s

(Whirlwinds), the best climbing speed was 55 knots and the best speed in descent of autorotation was 55 knots, so if they transgressed I only had to tap the ASI and say '*Peddy set-pet*' for them to get the message.

I was sent to Amman to give the Jordanian pilots a refresher course. While there I trained an RAF Wing Commander and I also gave King Hussein a refresher course. He had had training from a pilot who had never trained anyone before and he had not taught the king what to do in the event of engine failure (yes, I was appalled when I heard this), so I spent most of my time teaching him this and tidying up his flying generally. I received a watch from him too when I left. Unfortunately, I had to pay duty on it going through customs. I noted with annoyance that some RAF pilots who received the same gift some time later did not have to pay duty!

After a while the RAF sent their pilots for initial pilot training in smaller aircraft – either Bells or Hillers – I forget which. This was to save money. However, if the pilots thought that they just had to fly a bigger aircraft using the same techniques they had learnt, they were mistaken. Firstly, taking off was not just a matter of obtaining the correct rpm and then applying collective pitch; the Dragonfly hovered left wheel low and special techniques were needed to achieve take-offs and landings that look as if the pilot was in complete control. Secondly, and most importantly, whereas in small helicopters the pilot seldom needed to control the rotor rpm when in autorotation, in the larger helicopters he certainly did, especially when pulling out from a dive. In this case the rotor rpm would easily exceed the maximum unless the pilot increased collective pitch, and the amount used could often be surprisingly large.

I went on a tour of Spain and Portugal in an S-51 with Bill Hinks as salesman and John Coombes as the engineer. We went to Madrid in stages and when there I landed on the roof of a building. I also carried out a demonstration in the football ground of Real Madrid. Then on to Lisbon and Oporto for further demonstrations.

Another trip I did was to Cuba and Brazil. We had sold Cuba some S-55s. At the time Batista was running Cuba and Fidel Castro was a mere rebel hiding in the woods to the south-east of the country. Whilst a lot of things were pleasant there, for instance my hotel was right alongside a golden beach, life had its dark side. When Batista came to visit us, apart from shaking his hand, Keith Pardoe, our engineer, and I kept well away from him so as not to have our photographs taken with him. Then one day we went to the cinema to see *Bhowani Junction*. Fortunately we sat upstairs for we had seen only ten minutes of the film when a bomb went off in the stalls. I went forward and looked down expecting to see a mass of dead bodies, but the stalls were empty and there was nothing but metal seats torn apart by the explosion. Another time I was required to fly to hills in Castro country and demonstrate that the S-55 (Wasp engine and very underpowered) was capable of picking up at least one casualty. The landing site was surrounded by the sides of a wooded valley and I could visualise a sniper being able to pick us off very easily. In Rio de Janeiro I gave some instruction to Brazilian pilots in the Widgeon and also had a chance to hover near the Corcovado – the wonderful statue of Christ on the top of a mountain.

Building the S-51 (or Dragonfly) had been Westland's main occupation for several years and it introduced many people to the advantages of the helicopter, not least the military, and the Royal Navy was quick to order some.

Actually, the Royal Navy and RAF had been interested in helicopters for some time and my introduction to helicopters was made in 1944 when the Royal Navy possessed the Sikorsky R-4, or Gadfly (Hoverfly 1 in the RAF). At the time there were only three helicopters in the country. Contrast that with how many there are here today! Following the production of the Dragonfly Westland produced the Whirlwind S-55. After the Dragonfly this was a real workhorse with its much greater load-carrying capacity. They also produced the Widgeon, which was an amalgamation of the S-51 and the S-55. By this time, all the helicopters Westland produced had servo-operated controls; indeed, with the greater loads on the controls it would have been impossible to fly these larger helicopters without them.

An exception was the Bell 47-B-3 (or Sioux) that Westland produced later on as, being small, it had no need for servo controls and continued to have manually operated controls. After the piston-engined Whirlwind, Westland introduced a gas turbine version. With gas turbines the engine was controlled by computers and the pilot did not have to control the rpm all the time with a twist-grip throttle control. Then came the Wessex, which had a single, large Napier gas turbine engine; later versions had two smaller 'Gnome' gas turbines. This resulted in a very fine helicopter.

Westland also toyed with the idea of building the Hughes 269A, and one was sent over and bought by Westland. It was a very small aircraft with an interesting clutch system that consisted of a number of V belts which one tightened to engage. The aircraft itself was notable for descending at a very fast rate in autorotation. I had quite a lot to do with this Hughes and at one time I was sent to Libya to do some hot-weather trials with it.

In complete contrast to the Hughes, Westland thought in terms of very large helicopters and produced one Westminster – a large helicopter indeed – which looked just like a mass of plumbing gone wrong. I had one flight in it. Unfortunately, it was not thought to be viable and the project was dropped.

Jack Fraser, an Australian, joined the test pilot team and together with Derrick Colvin and Roy Bradley he flew the Wyvern, a fixed-wing aircraft. When British helicopter production became centred on Westland at Yeovil, the pilots and some aircraft were taken over from Bristol, Fairey and Saunders Roe. Thus we now had Peter Wilson, Ron Gellatly, John Morton, and also Ron Crayton, Roy Moxam, Leo De Vigne, Keith Chadbourn and Mike Ginn on the strength. 'Slim' Sear joined us as Chief Test Pilot and following him as chief were Ron Gellatly and then Roy Moxam. Hovercraft production and their pilots (if such is the correct term) were kept as a separate entity down in Cowes. Automatic pilots came into use during my time at Westland, although of course they are commonplace nowadays.

After Westland had taken over the Fairey Aviation Company, I had a chance to fly the Scout and the Wasp. Towards the end of my time I also had a couple of flights in the Sea King. I was delighted to see that this aircraft was still flying some 45 years after my time at Westland.

No chapter like this could be complete without mention of the Flight Test Observers. This title was later changed to Flight Test Engineers by John Speechley when he was Managing Director and it seemed a much more appropriate one. All of them operated as professional aircrew, and took their flying duties very seriously. I was always happy to have a second brain in the cockpit and much appreciated the work they did with their extensive knowledge of the design process and all things aeronautical. I remember them all with much appreciation.

20 Lynx – The Making of a Thoroughbred

David Gibbings

In 2011, Westland celebrated forty years since the Lynx flew for the first time. The aircraft represented the innovation and capability both in land-based and maritime roles, and proved to be a demonstration of the potential of the reconstructed British Helicopter industry.

As part of an Anglo-French three aircraft programme, it was also a glimpse into the future, where new designs would be produced by multi-national collaboration.

The following statement was produced for the programme distributed for RNAS Yeovilton Air Day staged in July 2011, which featured the Lynx as its central theme. This item is the longest single entry in this book but no excuse is offered for this; the story of what is a great British achievement should be told!

Flight Test Engineer David Gibbings first worked on the Lynx in 1967 as one of the team formulating the test plan. He remained with the project from the first flight to its entry into service with the Royal Navy and Army Air Corps. Flight-testing with the Lynx ran as a continuous thread throughout his working life; his last task on the day he retired from Westland, in 1993, was to take part in the acceptance flight of a Lynx off the production line.

Here he describes the background to the project and the events that have resulted in a great British helicopter.

Introduction

The Lynx helicopter is over forty years old, and yet it is difficult to visualise the Lynx as an old helicopter, as it has evolved in many ways incorporating integrated avionics, a complete reinstallation of a more powerful engine, which in turn has resulted in a spectacular improvement in performance.

There is always reluctance on the part of manufacturers to confess to the age of the aircraft they are trying to sell, but it is worth remembering that only good designs result in aircraft with long service lives. The Lynx was originally designed to meet requirements that faced the British Navy and Army at the height of the 'Cold War' in order to continue operations into the 1970s. The military staff requirement identified the need for a family of designs and the business aspects involved in meeting the demands led to the orders for an unprecedented number of aircraft.

Before embarking on the Lynx story it is worth looking at the way in which the military use of rotorcraft had developed in the two decades that had elapsed since the practical helicopter had become a reality. By the mid-1960s, all three services had begun to appreciate the potential of the helicopter, and required aircraft to replace their existing equipment for a number of reasons. There was a considerable amount of inter-service argument put forward regarding who should have what, and how the programme should be managed, and an insight into this activity will help set the scene.

Because it is the Senior Service, we will start with the Royal Navy.

The operation of aircraft from ships changed the concept and use of sea power forever. The attacks on Pearl Harbor and Taranto had demonstrated clearly that even the most formidable capital ships were vulnerable to a well-planned air attack.

The ability to use aviation to see over the horizon and deliver weapons meant that the accepted ideas of maritime forces, and the design of the ships necessary to maintain sea power, would need to be revised, and preconceived ideas regarding the deployment of ships changed beyond recognition.

The large capital ships with massive guns were no longer the primary weapon at sea, their place being taken by the aircraft carrier. The introduction of the submarine had already threatened to reduce the battleship's effectiveness and also to make it impossible for an island people to be fed. Here again, the use of aircraft was to prove to be an effective means of containing the submarine menace.

The years between the two world wars saw the growth of the aircraft carrier and with it Naval Aviation, but throughout the conflict, the deployment of aircraft required the availability of a floating base as large and as vulnerable as the dreadnoughts they replaced, albeit that the smaller warships such as cruisers could carry and operate seaplanes to enhance their range of vision. There was at this stage no possibility that destroyers or smaller ships could include aircraft as part of their armoury.

Rotorcraft and Small Ship Operations

The first practical rotorcraft were not in fact helicopters. Juan de la Cierva flew his first Gyroplane (Autogiro) in the mid-1920s, and although these unique aircraft could apparently hover given a headwind, they were not helicopters, and their deployment at sea was restricted by the limitations imposed to ensure safety.

The first ship landings with autogiros took place in Europe and USA during the early 1930s. The results indicated that it was possible to operate gyroplanes from ships, but that it was fraught with hazards, there was no enthusiasm for them and the world had to wait for a new vehicle.

This came towards the end of the Second World War, with the helicopter; here was a flying machine that could operate from a platform little larger than its own footprint.

There remained the issue of reliability and durability, and the infrastructure to maintain such machines was such that it outweighed the advantages. However, the stage was set.

The world's navies, and that must include the Royal Navy, were remarkably slow to fully appreciate the way in which the introduction of the helicopter could affect maritime warfare. Operations were centred on the aircraft carrier and the primary function confined to the role of rescue, but even here the deployment of helicopters brought about an immediate change to carrier operations.

It had been standard practice for a destroyer to follow the carrier during 'Flying Stations' to rescue aircrew from stricken aircraft, an all too frequent occurrence. The introduction of helicopters changed all this, making the aircraft carrier self-sufficient.

Once the operation of helicopters at sea had been accepted, attention turned to anti-submarine warfare. The escalation of the 'Cold War' was a defining moment, leading to the development of helicopters with the ability to seek and destroy submarines. The ASW helicopters were still carrier based when first introduced and as time progressed smaller ships such as cruisers were adapted to carry them.

Once the advantages had been realised, attention was finally turned to the operation of helicopters from small ships. With the realisation that it was necessary to develop the specialised helicopter capable of operating from small ships, a programme was launched using the Saunders-Roe P.531, and a series of trials carried out operating from an adapted destroyer, assessing a range of deck-landing undercarriages and deck-securing mechanisms, including skids, harpoons, winches, wheels, suckers, haul-down winches and short-term lashings.

It was as a result of these trials that a requirement was raised for a small helicopter with a strong wheeled undercarriage, which could allow its rotor and fuselage to be folded for stowage within small ships, and also the design would include the capability to apply negative collective pitch to hold it on the deck. The Wasp flew for the first time in 1963 and incorporated all these features; it was capable of carrying anti-submarine weapons, and for the first time the Royal Navy had a helicopter that was able to operate from vessels no bigger than a frigate, providing the capability to operate over the horizon without restricting the ship. The Wasp served the Royal Navy well, remaining in service until the mid-80s. It was, however, only an observation and weapon delivery platform; perhaps its legacy was that from it, the Royal Navy began to appreciate that a specialised helicopter capable of all-weather operations from small ships was a 'Force multiplier'.

There developed a clear understanding that any replacement for the Wasp would have to be larger, within the constraints imposed by the size of the ship, but also that the ship/helicopter operating limits, and the helicopter performance and handling would have to be improved.

In 1967, an incident occurred which threw all established thinking concerning maritime warfare into disarray. The Israeli destroyer *Eilat* was attacked by Egyptian (Russian-built) fast patrol boats and sank after receiving hits from 'Styx' missiles. The boats themselves had been designed to offer a low radar signature.

The fact that such a small force could dispatch a major warship, and that the incoming attack had not been detected in time, was cause for alarm.

The Royal Navy's requirement was modified to include anti-surface vessel capability with radar capable of detecting patrol boats, which had minimal radar signatures by design.

The experience gained with the Wasp was incorporated in the requirement NGAST 3335 from which the Lynx was to emerge.

Rotorcraft and Land Warfare

Aviation with the Army had for many years been confined to reconnaissance and artillery spotting. The exception here must be the use of gliders to deploy troops in large numbers, a form of warfare which came and went in the space of six years. However, army flying was still strongly influenced by the Royal Air Force, which maintained a considerable amount of control regarding operations and equipment, restricting the size of aircraft the Army could operate and totally opposing any armed aircraft.

The Army Air Corps became an independent service within the British Army in 1957, operating fixed-wing aircraft, primarily in the air observation role, but during this time the Skeeter was entering service and the potential of the helicopter was gradually realised.

By the early 1960s the Army Air Corps was beginning to appreciate the importance of the helicopter as a battlefield asset, and steps were in place to procure a Light Utility Helicopter (Scout) and a Unit Light Helicopter (Sioux), but there still remained a limit on the size of helicopter that the Army could operate (5,000lb AUW); this was strongly supported by the Royal Air Force, and for many years this policy inhibited the expansion of Army aviation.

The Vietnam War redefined the use of helicopters in support of land forces, and can be identified as a 'defining moment' in the evolution of helicopter usage and air mobility in the field. It became clear that the Army required an aircraft capable of carrying at least ten men, and should also carry some armament.

There was further understanding that within the 'Cold War' scenario, that it was vital for the Army to have control of its own anti-tank capability.

The Royal Air Force

The Royal Air Force was also slow to accept the introduction of helicopters. By the early '60s, an effective Search and Rescue service was in place around the UK, and the bigger twin-rotor Belvedere was in service. The mainstay of RAF operations was the Whirlwind.

The 'Malaysia confrontation' brought with it the realisation that, if it became necessary to support operation in remote areas or jungle, larger and reliable aircraft would be required.

With this increase in helicopter use in all three services, it became clear that there would also be a need for an advanced trainer.

Staff Requirement NGAST 3335 took in the interests of all three services, and was to lead to the Lynx.

The Response from Industry

In 1960, the British Aircraft Industry underwent a major reorganisation. The twenty or more separate companies, which had operated as separate manufacturers competing with each other, had been forced by government influence to amalgamate into larger groups, many famous names disappeared, and as a result the industry was reduced to two large groups: The British Aircraft Corporation and Hawker Siddeley Group.

The four helicopter companies were not included in the two large corporations, which remained dedicated to fixed-wing craft. The largest and by far more prosperous helicopter company was Westland Aircraft Company, which unlike the others had developed their business by building Sikorsky designs under licence. Such was their success that they were able to progressively acquire Bristol, Fairey and Saunders-Roe to form Westland Helicopters, and it was the restructured Westland Group that responded to the requirement.

All the companies that now comprised Westland had been engaged in project studies to meet perceived service requirements; with the new organisation came proposals incorporating the best from each of the original groups. One of these was the WG-3, which after several reappraisals resulted in the WG-13, and again after a number of revisions, this was offered as a response to NGAST 3335.

The Political Scene

It is impossible to ignore the political background against which new types of aircraft evolve.

The 1960s were a 'defining moment' for the procurement of helicopters for the British armed forces. Requirements for three distinctly different types of aircraft had been identified:

- An air portable tactical helicopter for the Royal Air Force.
- A light helicopter to serve as a unit light helicopter for the Army and also as a trainer for all three services.
- A medium-weight helicopter (approximately 8000lb all-up-weight) with a high performance, to provide a utility helicopter for the Army, capable of anti-tank warfare, and to provide the shipborne helicopter for the Royal Navy capable of operating from small ships and armed with anti-submarine weapons and also to deploy air-to-surface missiles to counter fast patrol boats.

The three requirements called for the procurement of over 200 helicopters, an unprecedented demand which would clearly call for more than the resources available within the Westland Group. The Government in power at the time was deeply involved in negotiations to consider the UK joining the Common Market (EEC). Although the possibility of UK membership was under negotiation, it was still well into the future. The completion of an Anglo-French agreement to produce the helicopters required would be seen as an indication of serious intentions on the part of the UK.

The French company Aerospatiale was already well advanced with the development programme for the SA-330, later to become the Puma, and it was considered that this aircraft would clearly meet most of the requirements for the tactical helicopter. Aerospatiale were also in the process of completing project studies for a light helicopter, which could also be considered for the unit light helicopter/trainer requirement.

A Westland WG-13 project study, aimed at fulfilling the requirements of both Army and Navy utility helicopters, could also be adapted to meet the French need for a similar aircraft. The Harold Wilson government was quick to appreciate that if a successful agreement could be made with one of the leading countries already within the Common Market, the possibility was that a British application for membership would be more favourably received. It was in fact considered to be very important that, of all the Common Market members, France should be behind a British application.

The Anglo-French Helicopter Package Deal was signed in February 1967. It was one of several international collaboration projects in being at the time, including Concorde and Jaguar.

There can be little doubt that the intention was for such projects to be seen as evidence that Britain was ready to join the international community.

From the industry's viewpoint they offered security in that although such deals were difficult to negotiate, they were even harder to stop once agreement had been registered.

Design Authority

The issue of Design Authority is fundamental to the engineering character of an aircraft. For many years up to the Second World War, the design could be credited to an individual designer: Spitfire/R.J. Mitchell, Hurricane/Sydney Camm.

As aircraft have become more complex, the design has been undertaken by teams, but within any company the ultimate responsibility still rests with a Chief Designer, who delegates his authority with care.

This process runs through the organisation as a sort of 'laying on of hands' and is intended to protect the integrity of the design.

In the case of an international project, the situation is complicated by the fact that, as part of the workshare, the design may be divided between two or even more companies, and this can be made even more complex by the differences that may exist in certification procedure.

In most cases this will invariably result in split design authority, and inevitably this can result in delay, and additional expense, simply because where quite small issues could normally be easily resolved at office level, it may well call for a meeting in another country. The Anglo-French deal was different from the other international projects at the time; the three aircraft involved were the subject of their own national design authorities.

Type	Company	Design Authority	Workshare	
Lynx	Westland	UK	70% UK	30% Fr
Puma	Aerospatiale	Fr	50% UK	50% Fr ★
Gazelle	Aerospatiale	Fr	50%UK	50% Fr ★

★ UK aircraft only

Based on the initial contracts alone, the Anglo-French deal would result in a colossal production commitment:

113 Lynx for the Army

86 Lynx for the RN

200 Gazelle for UK Forces

48 Puma for the RAF

'Intention to Proceed' was declared in July 1967

The Shaping of a New Helicopter

Prior to 1963 the four companies that comprised the British helicopter industry had all been working on their own interpretation of requirements for the British armed forces. Following the formation of Westland Helicopters Ltd, the project activities were brought together. This, however, took time, but by the end of 1963 the Westland Group was functioning well and the WG series of project studies was beginning to emerge. Project WG-3 was concerned with fulfilling the Army requirement in answer to General Staff Requirement GSR 3335, for a utility helicopter for the Army, capable of carrying ten men and operating in the field, detached from a fixed base. The WG-3 design went through several reappraisals over the period that followed, during which time the internal layout, overall size, all-up-weight, engine and transmission requirements were discussed and changed frequently.

By 1965 the requirements for the Royal Navy were beginning to influence project thinking, and it was quickly appreciated that the overall configuration of the aircraft required for maritime operations was not dissimilar to that required for the Army. Much of the discussion centred around inter-service arguments. Not surprisingly the Army would be satisfied with a reasonably large aircraft, which the Royal Air Force considered excessive, while the Royal Navy made it clear that the aircraft they required would have to operate from ships, which at the time were operating Wasps. Around this time the idea of an international collaborative requirement was beginning to emerge, and the introduction of an armed reconnaissance helicopter (maybe even a gunship) was brought into the equation.

Project WG-13 began to address all the arguments and considerations for an aircraft that would satisfy requirements for the Army and maritime operation, with the ability to produce an armed attack variant incorporating the main features such as rotor system and transmission.

The Joint Service Requirement (NGAST 3335) was issued in June 1966. This document accepted the need for a multi-variant design to meet the requirements of the Army and for maritime operations. Provision was also included to provide for the armed attack variant that would draw heavily on the basic design for its main mechanical features: power system, gearbox, rotor head and blades.

There were twenty-four identifiable variations of the WG-13 (WG-13A to WG-13X) in being before the final configuration of the WG-13 was revealed in the summer of 1966. By the summer of 1967 the main elements of the requirement were agreed, the necessary management structure for the Anglo-French agreement was put in place and specifications were available at least in draft form, sufficient to allow design, forward ordering of materials and initial development planning and testing to commence.

What's in a Name?

Throughout most of its design phase the new aircraft was known as WG-13, but there was an immediate interest in the name for an aircraft that could well endure into the twenty-first century.

Westland favoured a name commencing with 'W', and at one stage the name 'Witch' appeared to be in favour. Perhaps it is not surprising that nobody has actually claimed credit for this, and there was general relief when a naming competition was announced; members from the three services, MoD and Industry were all eligible.

The rules were:
   The name had to be bi-lingual.
   Names commencing with 'W' would be favoured.
   The chosen name should be able to accept the prefix 'Sea', as in Sea Fury.

The competition attracted wide interest throughout the industry and the armed forces, all of whom were eligible to take part, and a prize of £75 was promised for the winner.

A vast number of names were offered, including 'Wildcat'.

There were seventeen submissions suggesting 'Lynx'. This was widely favoured because there was already a trend evolving to name joint projects after the wild animals, such as Jaguar, Puma and Gazelle.

The response to the competition was much larger than expected; the committee finally awarded the princely sum of £5 to each of the lucky seventeen.

The WG-13 Lynx

So it was that the Lynx was accepted to fill the requirement for a light utility helicopter for the Army, and for a helicopter capable of operating from small ships for the Royal Navy. The Royal Air Force withdrew. The basic requirements were as follows:

Army Utility Helicopter

All-up weight 8000lb
Max sustained speed 160 knots
Roles: Reconnaissance
         Command post
         Liaison in forward areas
         Anti-tank
         Personnel and equipment supply
         Casualty Evacuation

Royal Navy, Small Ships Helicopter

All-up weight 8000lb
Max sustained speed 145 knots
Roles: Anti-submarine (classify and attack)
      Surface search
      Anti-surface vessel
      Transport of personnel
      Search-and-rescue (SAR)
      Vertical replenishment

Airframe

The basic configuration of the Lynx was that of a conventional helicopter, with a four-blade main rotor and single tail rotor. The Lynx airframe was of light alloy stressed skin construction with large sliding doors each side of the cabin. Access for the aircrew was gained through two hinged doors on either side. Aft of the aircrew seats the main cabin floor was unobstructed and incorporated tie-down links. Removable seating was available to carry ten fully equipped troops and provision was to be made for armament. The non load-carrying structures such as doors and fairings made extensive use of composite materials and Nomex honeycomb; the application of composites for aircraft structures was in its infancy at the time. The landing gear for the Army aircraft consisted of the simple fixed skid undercarriage of rugged construction, designed for simplicity and ease of maintenance.

The naval aircraft required an undercarriage, which was an integral part of the deck landing system. A conventional tricycle nose wheel landing gear was chosen with the three wheels centred around the deck securing device. The system was designed specifically to allow safe operation from small ships, permitting rotation of the aircraft so that take-off and landing could be made into favourable wind conditions independently of the ship's heading.

Provision was made for a deck lock system capable of restraining the aircraft on the deck but with the wheels suitably arranged to allow rotation about the deck lock. The basic oleo unit was common for all three of the wheel installations. The main undercarriage carried single wheels, which could be positioned manually to allow rotation. The nose undercarriage carried twin wheels and could be castored by the pilot. The main wheels were fitted with wheel locks, which when engaged prevented rotation, and could be operated from within the cockpit or externally by the handling crew. The whole installation was structurally strong enough to withstand the high loads and harsh conditions imposed by a ship at sea.

The Rotor Head and Blades

The semi-rigid (hingeless) rotor head was arguably the most technically advanced and innovative feature introduced into the Lynx design, the only hinge in the system being the blade feathering hinge, all movement in flap and lag taken by two flexible elements.

The rotor hub is forged from a single block of titanium forming the hub centre, with the four flapping element arms extruded to form the centre pivot for the feathering hinge. Flexibility in the lag plane is achieved by the titanium outboard arm which is of circular cross-section. This provides movement in the lag plane, and carries the sleeve of the feathering hinge, and the control attachment arm at its inboard end; the outboard end carries the lugs for blade attachment by means of two bolts.

The rotor head design provided a degree of agility and responsive handling, with good reliability and ease of maintenance. It was ideally suited for ship operations, but also resulted in agility and reliability on the battlefield.

The main rotor blades consisted of a stainless steel spar with composite rear pockets, which were reinforced with a 'Nomex' honeycomb interior, a high-performance cambered aerofoil section was chosen, all of which resulted in an agile and responsive aircraft. A small crew could fold the blades manually.

Provision for Deck Operations

The small ship environment from which the Lynx would have to operate demanded that the aircraft could be housed and maintained in the smallest possible space. The maritime aircraft included a manual tailfold for this reason.

The aircraft is fitted with four main lashing points, one at the end of each sponson attached to the mainwheel leg. There are two forward points situated in front of the cockpit on the nose bulkhead strongpoint. The key item in the whole deck landing process is the 'Decklock System'. This comprises a hydraulically operated retractable 'harpoon type' decklock situated in a central position in the aircraft's floor structure. It can be selected by the pilot to engage with a 2.5m/8.2ft grid in the ship's deck to secure the helicopter with a nominal force of 3000lb; the decklock would be released by the pilot for lift-off. The other important feature for the deck landing requirement is the ability to apply up to 6° of negative collective pitch after landing, allowing the pilot to hold and control the aircraft firmly in position on the deck until harpoon engagement has been accomplished, but also to facilitate landings on ships that may not have harpoon grids.

The items that comprise the deck landing system are those that have made the Lynx foremost as a small ships' operation, giving the Lynx an unrivalled capability for operation from small ships at sea in high sea states and ship motion. All of this has been achieved without the need for elaborate securing systems other than the provision of a harpoon grid.

Transmission System

The Lynx requirement called for reliability and low overall height, a feature that was important for ease of stowage, battlefield security and transportability. The resultant gearbox system was elegant in design and compact.

In keeping with the policy of adopting state-of-the-art technology, the main ring gear driving the main rotor used conformal gear profiles, which offered improved gear contact and lubrication, with superior load carrying capability. The transmission system followed conventional helicopter practice, driving the tail rotor through a third pinion from the main conformal ring gear, via intermediate and tail gearboxes. Accessories such as alternators, hydraulics and gearbox lubrication were all driven through a conventional accessory drive system situated at the front of the main gearbox.

Power Plant

The engine selected for the Lynx was the Rolls-Royce BS 360 (later to be named 'Gem'). This was a new engine featuring a two-spool gas generator section and two-stage free power turbine.

Max continuous power	750shp
Intermediate contingency & five-minute rating	830shp
Max contingency	900shp

The above power ratings represent the situation at the outset of the programme, and have increased as the aircraft and engine have developed.

Avionics Systems

The avionics fit specified for the Lynx at the time was to a very advanced standard. Technology has moved at an unbelievable pace and the development of the Lynx has reflected this and will be even more evident in the Wildcat.

The Lynx as offered in response to NGSAR 3335 was as follows:
Honeywell Radio Altimeter (linked to AFCS)
Decca Type 71 Doppler Radar
Decca Tactical Air Navigation System (TANS)
Ferranti Sea Spray Radar
IFF
Four-axis Automatic Flight Control System, providing the following:

Heading Hold & Trim	Transition to Hover
Radio & Barometric Height Hold	Doppler Hover

The Integrated Test Programme

Work began in earnest in 1967, a Project Definition Study existed and the task to develop a new helicopter began. This entailed:

The advance ordering of materials.
Selection of subcontractors.
Identification of 'high risk' items.
The integration of delivery dates for key items to achieve first flight.
Deciding the number of test rigs and aircraft to achieve the programme.
Setting up the infrastructure for component tests and instrumentation.
Formulating an integrated Development Test Programme.

It must be remembered that although computers were available to undertake some of the tasks, information technology was in its infancy, computers were large, expensive, and in general only available for the most urgent tasks. There were management tools available, and one of these, which was known by the acronym 'PERT' (the age of the acronym was about to begin), was used to support the programme.

At working level, we all relied on our trusty slide rules, with resort to calculating machines where necessary.

Preliminary Testing

It was important to get the test programme under way; already work was in hand to assess the characteristics of new materials such as titanium, and the process of selecting instrumentation was in hand.

In addition to the prototype aircraft, there was a need for ground test rigs, some of which required representative airframes for the task. The call for airframes meant that a mini production line was necessary, and this was complicated by the fact that each rig and test airframe had its own individual build standard.

The requirement for airframe rigs and prototype aircraft was as follows:

Airframe Rigs

Rotor Rig	This was the principal rotor test rig/airframe and was sited at RNAS Yeovilton
Impedance Test Airframe	Fully representative airframe for resonance
Basic/Utility Fatigue Airframe	Fatigue Test airframes
Naval Fatigue Airframe	Fatigue Test airframes

Basic/Utility Static Test Airframe	Structural Test airframes
Naval Static Test Airframe	Structural Test airframes

Prototype aircraft

The Flight Test Programme involved a total of thirteen aircraft:

Ser No		1st Flight	
WG13-00-01	XW835	21-3-71	Basic Prototype
WG13-00-02	XW836	24-3-72	Basic Prototype
WG13-00-03	XW837	28-9-71	Basic Prototype
WG13-00-04	XW838	9-3-72	Basic Prototype
WG13-00-05	XW839	19-6-74	Basic Prototype
WG13-00-RR	XX907	20-5-73	Basic Aircraft/Engine Development
WG13-01-01	XX153	12-4-72	Utility (ARMY) Prototype
WG13-03-01	XX904	6-7-73	Aeronavale Prototype (F-ZKCU)
WG13-03-02	XX911	18-9-73	Aeronavale Prototype (F-ZKCV)
WG13-05-01	XX469	25-5-72	Naval Prototype
WG13-05-02	XX510	5-3-73	Naval Prototype
WG13-05-03	XX910	23-4-74	Royal Navy Prototype
WG13-05-04	XX166	5-3-75	Royal Navy Prototype

As can be seen, the build programme entailed the manufacture of nineteen airframes, each built without the benefit of a common production process, each with its own unique build standard, all influenced by changes brought about as the flying programme called for modifications, a major undertaking in its own right.

In addition to the aircraft and airframes there were a number of Systems Rigs, which although not housed in an airframe did entail representative equipment fit:

Hydraulic System Rig
Electrical System Rig
Landing Gear Drop Test Rig
NGTE Icing Rig

Rotor Head Demonstrator

The bold decision to adopt the semi-rigid rotor head for the Lynx was identified as a high-risk area, and it was considered necessary to gain experience at the earliest possible opportunity. With this in mind, a scaled-down version of the design was manufactured and installed in a Scout helicopter.

The opportunity to gain experience with the new rotor would be extremely valuable, making it possible to assess ground resonance, response, handling qualities, vibration characteristics and to establish test and analysis techniques in advance of the test programme with the definitive system. It was decided to modify two aircraft, one for the assessment by the manufacturer for the Lynx programme, and the other to be used by the Royal Aircraft Establishment for rotor research.

The first modified aircraft (Scout XP189) was available for testing early in 1970 and work commenced to undertake ground resonance testing on a specially prepared tie-down base. The test followed a well-established procedure whereby the helicopter was placed, freestanding, secured by cables attached to strong points directly under the rotor head. The aircraft was unrestrained during running and the full range of stress and vibration data were available to an operator in the secure control cabin. If the instrumentation indicated any resonant tendencies, cables could be tensioned hydraulically to restrain the aircraft.

The comprehensive programme covering a range of rotor speeds and power settings was carried out without event until the task was almost complete, when divergent resonance was observed with the aircraft running at flight-idle. Analysis showed instability in lag and immediate design action was taken to fit lag dampers across the lag element, which proved successful; action was taken to include lag damping in the Lynx head.

This one incident justified the inclusion of the Scout exercise, which continued to prove the concept of the semi-rigid rotor head and provide invaluable experience to the engineering staff and test crew in advance of the main flight programme.

The modified aircraft was re-assessed and cleared for flight, which took place on 31 August 1970. Some twenty-five hours of flying was completed, sufficient to give confidence that the Lynx Programme could proceed. The second Research Scout, XP191, continued flying at RAE Bedford.

The Lynx Development Programme

The formal declaration of 'Intention to Proceed', which was to signal commencement of the development programme, was announced in July 1967. Until this time, all work on the WG-13 project by the company had been undertaken on trust. Work now began to design the aircraft in detail, and commence the vast range of integrated tests of equipment and sub-systems necessary to allow first flight.

Instrumentation

The instrumentation installation represents the payload of any test aircraft. Before commencement on any test programme, the way in which data is gathered and processed has to be determined and the essential equipment ordered. This not only entails the instrumentation fit in the aircraft, but also the whole range of test facilities throughout the factory, and also has to include the way in which results are analysed. The selection of an instrumentation system for a major project entails not only ensuring that the manufacturers are covered, but it is also important that whatever system is used is compatible with that employed by subcontractors and the certification authority.

It is important that operators and a flight-test aircrew are thoroughly familiar with the equipment and able to deal with in-flight re-loads and simple troubleshooting. Each aircraft is allocated specific tasks such as performance, handling or stress measurement. Each of these may call for a different combination of instrumentation and many of the sensors may need to be situated in inaccessible areas of the airframe during build. It was decided at an early stage to ensure that all the development aircraft would include wiring provision to allow conversion for stress measurements if required.

At the time when the Lynx programme commenced, telemetry was becoming a feature of many flight test organisations, and it was decided to investigate the installation of telemetry. The system was selected and telemetry was a feature of all-important trials with the Lynx from 1974 onwards.

Main Rotor Head

The titanium semi-rigid rotor head was one of the advanced technology features which was totally new to Westland or Aerospatiale experience. The manufacture of the rotor head was part of the workshare allocated to SNIAS.

The first rotor heads were manufactured with the flapping elements bolted separately into the central hub. This approach was chosen so that flapping elements could be changed quickly should it be found necessary to change to flapping frequency. The first twelve months the programme were all carried out with bolted rotor heads using the first two aircraft.

The MacRobert Award

In 1975 the design team for the Lynx gearbox and rotor head received the MacRobert Award from the Royal Academy of Engineering in recognition of the innovation brought about by the introduction of conformal gears and the semi-rigid rotor.

The named recipients were: D.E.H. Balmford, K.T. McKenzie, G.J. Smith-Pert, J. Speechley and V.A.B. Rogers.

The Rolls-Royce BS 360 (Gem) Power Plant

Most Flight Test Engineers will agree that developing the new engine in parallel with a new aircraft should be avoided, and yet time and again this seems to happen, as it did with the Lynx, to the extent that by the time the first flight was ready it was predicted that the test engines would only have a twenty-five-hour engine life. There was therefore a need to plan for the provision of engines in sufficient numbers to support the high flying rate necessary to achieve the programme's objectives.

The first engines were delivered for the rotor rig, to be followed by the flight units for the prototype aircraft. It is important that the development of the new engine should not be hurried simply to meet the flight programme. The consequence was that for the first year the availability of engines was not adequate and it became necessary to delay the first flight of the third aircraft, and in many cases it was necessary to move engines from one aircraft to another to keep the programme running smoothly. As the engine gained maturity, the situation eased.

The Rotor Rig

One of the most important facilities available to the programme was the rotor rig, which was sited at Yeovilton. The rig was to all intents and purposes a fully serviceable aircraft firmly fixed to the ground. The intention was that running time and component lives would always be ahead of that achieved by any of the test aircraft.

The rig was maintained and run to aircraft standards so that any components installed on the rig would be acceptable for use on an aircraft. An important function was to place items such as rotor blades onto the rig and they were subjected to tests in advance of their use in flight.

The rig was run for the first time in September 1970 and continued to support the flight programme for several years. The importance of the rotor rig to the programme cannot be overstated. Not only was it successful as a means of ensuring the integrity of major components such as an rotor blades and transmission, but it also provided opportunity for the pilots to operate and understand the aircraft.

The Flight Programme

Painted bright yellow, the Lynx prototype (XW835) flew for the first time on Sunday 21 March 1971. The pilot, Ron Gellatly, completed two short flights (10 and 20 min duration each). Short flights of this nature at the start of testing are typical with initial flights for helicopters, because of the possibility of oil leaks from the transmission.

In addition to Ron Gellatly, his deputy, Roy Moxam occupied the co-pilot's seat, and Dave Gibbings flew as the flight test engineer, responsible for instrumentation management, stress data monitoring and back-up observations.

Both of the flights were carried out close to the airfield and sufficient work was done to give confidence that a flight for the press could be arranged for the following day.

The build standard for the initial flight programme was uncomplicated, but fully representative. The engines were to a very early standard with low power ratings and a declared engine life of only twenty-five running hours, the definitive rotor blades were not available, and early flying was carried out using Wessex blades cropped to the appropriate length.

One of the most important features for assessment was the semi-rigid rotor head. The chosen design represented the forefront of rotor technology, and it was expected to result in the Lynx establishing a substantial lead in the handling qualities necessary for ship operations.

The rotor heads on the first two aircraft consisted of a steel central hub, the four titanium flapping elements bolted in position. Adjustment to the dynamic characteristics of the rotor could call for the removal of metal from the flexible elements.

The production rotor head would feature a central hub with four integral flapping elements forged from a single block of titanium; known as the 'monobloc' head, this was the standard chosen for production.

It must be confessed that the vibration levels experienced on the early flights were very high. It has to be appreciated that vibration is an ever present feature of helicopter flight, and a considerable amount of testing is usually devoted to bringing this to an acceptable level. The most apparent vibration frequency experienced on a helicopter is generally that induced by the rotor, but this is often affected by the tail rotor and by the natural frequency of the structure.

The Lynx was no exception; the rotor frequency levels were high, and there were a number of higher frequency levels coupled with structural response that required attention. A great deal of effort was put into vibration measurement, aimed at achieving a satisfactory level for safety and, of course, crew comfort.

The results are generally achieved by changes in structure or component mountings, and sometimes by damping critical components. Often, having improved the situation in one area, things are made worse in others, and of course people also vibrate! This manifested itself in the early days with the famous 'Lynx nose itch', a persistent high frequency irritation, which would not go away, but did not affect everybody to the same degree.

However, we all suffered for England, and as time progressed the Lynx structure was refined to result in an acceptable ride. The assessment and improvement of vibration levels is a complex subject, and remains a major consideration in helicopter design.

The basic Lynx development was carried out using five prototype aircraft, each of which was painted a different colour:

XW835 Yellow
XW836 Grey
XW837 Red
XW838 Blue
XW839 Orange

There has never been an explanation for the reasoning behind this, but it did turn out to be extremely useful when waiting for your aircraft to be put up for flight, or if one was about one's business in the offices; a glimpse from the window was enough to determine which aircraft was on the approach and decide whether to hurry back for the debrief. Someone was heard to say that it made the flight pad look like a snooker frame or a box of 'Smarties'.

Fuselage and cabin vibration levels proved to be a big problem and a great deal of time and effort was expended to improve the situation. There followed a programme where an aircraft was progressively stiffened in specific areas, by the introduction of steel support members (in fact, industrial RSJ sections were used).

There were some fifteen or more different schemes assessed, and some of these were tested together, so there were occasions when the whole rear of the aircraft was unusable. In the event, the modifications concerned that were adopted were: stiffening in the rear cabin, milled frame area, stiffer engine decking and two support rods across the angled section of the tail boom; these were known as the 8c struts, and they have remained with the aircraft throughout its service career. There was a period when the first aircraft was withdrawn from flight and used for a series of static tests, which entailed suspending the aircraft with its skids clear of the ground while vibration inputs were applied.

Engine life remained a persistent problem throughout the first year of testing, because of the short engine life. Most prototype engines fail to achieve their declared engine life, and Rolls-Royce had difficulty meeting the requirement. There was consequently a shortfall of six engines, and one of the development aircraft was in fact laid up for a long period. The flying programme was maintained by moving engines between aircraft to undertake specific tasks.

The stability arising from the tail design was investigated and at one stage the Lynx was flying with a large single underfin, and an inverted 'V' was also assessed.

In March 1972 the fourth basic aircraft flew for the first time and it included the first 'monobloc' rotor head. This was in fact the aircraft nominated to undertake the stress data gathering programme, which could now begin what is arguably one of the most important tasks in the programme. By the end of May 1972 the prototype utility (Army) and the first Naval aircraft had flown, and there were now six aircraft available to the programme, two of which could undertake tasks related to their operational use.

The general performance and handling of the Lynx proved to be well up to expectations and it was considered important to demonstrate these qualities to the world in order to encourage sales. In June 1972 the utility aircraft set a world speed record of 199.92mph, and as testing progressed it became clear that the Lynx possessed excellent handling qualities and response. In order to demonstrate this a series of manoeuvring tests were carried out culminating in the aircraft showing itself to be capable of aerobatic manoeuvres. At the 1972 SBAC show both the Army and the naval aircraft demonstrated rolling and looping.

The Development of the Naval Aircraft

The availability of the first definitive naval aircraft was a major milestone in the programme. The aircraft XX469 was flown for the first time by Westland Test Pilot John Morton on 25 May 1972.

The new aircraft was subjected to a schedule to determine basic performance, handling, stress data levels, vibration and systems functioning, in preparation for ship interface trials to commence. Assessment of the deck landing capability began with a comprehensive series of trials using the rolling platform facility at RAE Bedford. This was a large rig with a representative ships' helipad capable of reproducing the ship's rolling and pitching motion. Not only was it possible to assess the flight aspects of deck landing, but it was also possible to check the ability to work around an active aircraft on a moving deck for attachment of short-term lashings and to undertake servicing operations, such as engine change, blade fold or engine running. The rolling platform trials were a great success and preparation was made to take the Lynx to sea.

In November 1972, XX469 was severely damaged following the failure of the tail fold mechanism while in a low hover on the airfield at Yeovil. The two crew members received minor injuries, but the aircraft was category 5 and was lost to the programme. The loss of XX469 was a major setback, and immediate steps were taken to ensure that an aircraft was available to continue. The second naval prototype XX510 was brought forward and flew on 5 March 1973, and during the summer of that year it was based at the Aerospatiale site at Marignane to undertake performance and handling trials and ship trials using the French Navy frigate *Tourville*.

Another important aspect for the naval variant was the installation of the Sea Spray radar. These tests were carried out with both aircraft operating over Lyme Bay. Testing was constantly interrupted by the presence of Russian surveillance trawlers, which regularly operated off Portland, engaged in electronic data gathering. Whenever these were operative, the radar was switched off.

The radar trials culminated in assessment against fast patrol boats. Separate tests were also undertaken to ensure that the Sea Skua air-to-surface missile would be available in time for service. By the summer of 1974, aircraft XX910 and XZ166 had joined the programme. The first production Naval Lynx XZ227 flew for the first time on 10 February 1976, and the first delivery to the Royal Navy was made on 8 July 1976.

The development programme to provide the basic naval aircraft was accomplished in the space of four years. The Royal Netherlands Navy ordered the Lynx before the UK trials were complete and the first Lynx Mk 25 (UH-14A) flew in September 1976, and RNN aircraft were delivered in parallel with RN aircraft.

The Intensive Flying Trials Unit No700L NAS was formed in September 1976. This unit was unique in that it included aircraft and personnel from the Royal Netherlands Navy, working to achieve a service release for both services. The Lynx entered service with the Royal Navy on 26 January 1978 when No702 NAS was commissioned.

The Army Lynx

Development of the utility Lynx for the Army was carried out in parallel with the naval aircraft; much of the detail was in fact common to both variants, and often required little more than confirmation. Although there was in fact only one dedicated Army prototype, the five basic prototypes closely represented the Army configuration and a great deal of the vehicle aspect work was carried out using these machines.

Not everything went according to plan; there were incidents, which resulted in delays, that sometimes necessitated repairs and even lost aircraft to the programme.

During the initial phase, XW835 suffered a turbine failure and fire, requiring an emergency landing. The fire was contained but the damage was such that the aircraft was out of circulation for over twelve months.

When it did return it was fitted with PT-7 engines to prepare for possible civil use, and carried the civil registration G-BEAD.

Naval aircraft XX469 has already been discussed, and Basic aircraft XW838 suffered a tail rotor failure in the hover during an assessment of a proposal to reverse the rotor, and was lost to the programme.

None of the above incidents resulted in serious injury to the flight crews, but it did mean loss of aircraft. And as it turned out, all three of these were primarily concerned with stress data gathering. The stress measurements call for a very detailed and unique instrumentation fit, which is generally put in as part of the aircraft's build.

The possibility that stress aircraft might be lost had been considered during the planning stage, and arrangements made that all the development aircraft could be quickly brought into use.

This attention to detail typifies the approach to safety and contingency built into the programme.

The Utility prototype XX153 was used for handling, radio trials and role assessment.

The Lynx also carried TANS (Tactical Air Navigation System), a Doppler-driven navigation computer, which at the time was considered to be state of the art.

The Lynx carried no built-in anti-icing or de-icing system, but trials were carried out to assess the 'flight in icing capability' and icing limitations were declared.

The first production Lynx AH Mk1 XZ170 flew on 1 February 1977 and deliveries to the Army Air Corps commenced the following June, and by the end of the year Lynx was deployed in Germany.

The French Navy (Aeronavale)

The basic development of the French Naval aircraft was carried out as part of the UK-based Lynx programme and the Anglo-French package deal. The first two French aircraft, XX904 and XX911, were retained at Yeovil to undertake specific trials until deliveries to the French Navy commenced in September 1978.

Weight Growth

The Lynx was conceived as a maritime or utility aircraft with an all-up weight of 8,000lb.

The Lynx AH Mk 1 entered service with an all-up weight of 8,800lb, and as new roles and equipment have been introduced this has grown to 11,300lb (Lynx AH Mk 9).

The Lynx HAS Mk 2 entered service with an all-up weight of 9,750lb, and it too has been subject to weight growth to 11,750lb (Lynx HAS Mk 8).

The progressive increase in performance and capability has been possible because of improvements in several areas:

1. Engine development; the power available from the Rolls-Royce Gem engine has increased from 900shp (Gem 20) to 1,140shp (Gem 42). The introduction of the LHTEC T800 in the Lynx AH Mk 9A provides 1,340shp.
2. The introduction of BERP main rotor blades.
3. Transmission improvements.

The Company Lynx Demonstrator (G-LYNX)

The entry into service with the UK armed forces, and the fact that even at this stage the aircraft was already entering service with the Royal Netherlands Navy, gave confidence that further export orders would follow; this being so, it was clear that some customers would be demanding equipment or weapons that had not been cleared as part of the current UK clearance.

In order to conduct trials outside the requirements of the MoD, a trials aircraft would be required. Westland also recognised a need for an aircraft directly under their control for sales demonstrations.

A Lynx Mk 1 (Army variant), the 102nd airframe off the production line, was acquired for this purpose and registered in the Westland company's name with the civil registration G-LYNX, and flew for the first time in 1979.

The aircraft was extensively used from the outset to test armament and avionic equipment for export customers, and it was also the test vehicle for the LHTEC T800 engines, but perhaps its most well-known achievement occurred in 1986 when Trevor Egginton and Flight Test Engineer Derek Clews claimed the absolute world speed record for helicopters by flying over a 15km course at 249.1mph/400.87kph.

The record has stood for twenty-five years, during which time the Lynx has justified its claim to be 'the fastest helicopter in the world'.

The British Experimental Rotor Programme (BERP)

The BERP rotor blades (which must qualify for the world's worst acronym) were a key factor in the successful record attempt. Like most helicopter companies, Westland had recognised the advantages of composite blades and were certain that the precision achievable using their composite fabrication techniques would result in improved performance.

The record attempt was undertaken to demonstrate Westland's blade capability.

Export Lynx

As expected, export orders for the Lynx began to materialise. Sixteen nations operate the Lynx, requiring the aircraft for a range of different roles:

Anti-Submarine

Anti Surface Vessel

Search and Rescue

Coastguard

Utility Transport

Maritime Support (small ships helicopter)

Reconnaissance

Product Improvement

The Lynx has kept pace with the advances in technology, none more so than with avionics. The improvements brought about to produce the HAS Mk 8 transformed the Lynx and have paved the way for the Wildcat.

The introduction of infra-red (PID), glass cockpit and central tactical system, not only gave the Royal Navy a more effective asset but prompted requests for similar improvements from other operators where new aircraft were required.

Some operators elected to undertake major upgrades to their existing fleets, including re-airframing and life extension.

The year 2011 was the 40th anniversary of the first flight of the Lynx prototype and the 25th anniversary of the successful record attempt. As part of the celebrations, AgustaWestland apprentices have carefully restored G-LYNX to its speed record trim.

The aircraft is now on show at the Helicopter Museum, Weston-super-Mare. A tribute to a great British achievement, and a great helicopter.

Life begins at 40

The Lynx flew for the first time over forty years ago. It can arguably claim to be the most capable small ship's helicopter in the world, and demonstrably the fastest!

It has also demonstrated that it is a valuable military asset, proven in battle, and few would doubt that it will remain in service for some time to come.

Its successor, the Wildcat, inherits many of its best features, and as that too matures in service, it will continue to be recognised as a can-do helicopter.

It began with the Scout and Wasp, and will continue into the foreseeable future.

That's a pedigree of which, all of us, whether we built it, or operated it, can be proud.

21 The Procurement Dilemma

David Gibbings

When Westland started at the beginning of the First World War even the largest aircraft, the Vickers Vimy, cost less than £5,000. Fifty years later a Sea King costs several million pounds. And the cost of a Merlin has escalated even further.

The higher cost reflects the complexity of the on-board systems, which in turn extends the duration of the test programme. The result is that the defence scenario for which the new aircraft was ordered may have changed drastically.

The Merlin and Apache are good examples, explained by David Gibbings.

It is well understood that once a new weapon system has become established in squadron service, it is necessary to start considering its replacement. By the late 1970s the Sea King had been in service with the Royal Navy for ten years and already undergone several service updates, and although it clearly had a long service life ahead of it, the time was right to consider its replacement.

In 1977 Naval Staff Requirement 6646 was issued, detailing a substantially larger aircraft to carry the next generation of ASW equipment, with increased performance and capability.

Westland responded with WG 34; considerably heavier than the Sea King but with the added complexity of small ship capability, it quickly became apparent that to answer the UK requirement in isolation would be prohibitively expensive and so it was decided to look for an international partner with a similar requirement.

The Italian Navy was already operating a derivative of the Sea King manufactured under licence by Agusta, and was in the process of drawing up a requirement for its replacement.

Westland had previously worked successfully with Agusta in the 1960s to produce the Sioux, following a series of inter-company discussions; the British and Italian governments signed a Memorandum of Understanding (MOU 1) in November 1979. This action led to the formation of a joint company, in June 1980, named European Helicopter Industries (EHI), to manage the development, production and marketing of the new helicopter, to be designated EH-101, intended not only to respond to the maritime requirement, but also for civil and military transport applications.

It is worth considering the political scene at this time. Soviet Russia was the primary threat, and in particular the containment of submarine activities from northern bases; the Berlin Wall was in place and the central European plain was seen as a possible battlefield; Saddam Hussein, if not our ally was at least accepted as a trading partner; whilst Yugoslavia was seen as a viable and cohesive nation.

The situation in the Middle-East was at least in a state of armed stability.

Such was the environment against which the requirement for the new helicopter was drawn up, and this typifies the dilemma for those charged with procurement of equipment which even with a fair wind is unlikely to be in service in less than a decade from the point at which a decision is made.

The 1980s were also a defining moment in technical development with regard to rotor design, materials and, in particular, avionics. The new generation of helicopters would be software driven to an extent hitherto unthought of, demanding new skills of designers and managers.

In June 1981, the project definition phase was entered, the requirement for the two navies was laid down, and the tough negotiations regarding allocation of workshare were resolved. Over the two years that followed, much of the design work was undertaken, the avionic design representing as much as fifty per cent of the effort.

The workshare issue was in itself interesting. Westland was keen to undertake a significant part of the avionics task, but to take it on in its entirety would preclude full involvement with the airframe design. For Westland to maintain its place as a platform manufacturer, and in particular to ensure that the world-beating BERP blade technology was retained, it was necessary to compromise. Agusta was very keen to undertake the transmission. The workshare discussions were, to say the least, interesting, but it is a measure of the way in which the two companies were able to work that an acceptable plan was evolved.

In 1984, MOU 3 giving the full go-ahead for the design and development was signed, and manufacture of the preproduction aircraft commenced (nine in all, four in Italy and five in the UK). The first aircraft (PP-1) flew from Yeovil in October 1987, quickly followed by PP-2 in Italy in November; by 1990 eight aircraft were flying on the programme.

As early as 1988 it became apparent that some important aspects of the basic development such as performance, handling and stress data gathering would be best served by operating the appropriate aircraft from a single site. The fact that the main transmission items were produced and maintained in Italy, coupled with the climate and availability of high-altitude test sites, resulted in PP-1 joining PP-2 at Cascina Costa, where a joint Westland and Agusta team worked together for two years.

It is generally accepted that one should avoid developing a new aircraft with a power unit which is itself under development. In the case of the EH-101, the original specification called for three 1,279shp CT-7 engines, so we thought we had got away with it. However, halfway through the programme it was decided that the UK military aircraft would have the new 2,100shp RTM-322. Plans were put in place to install the new engines in PP-4 and PP-5, and the additional installation lay-ups and integration work added to the already tight programme.

Other specification changes included a late decision to include dunking sonar in the RN aircraft.

Complex flight test programmes are not without their hazards; two aircraft were lost, one (PP-2) in Italy with catastrophic loss of life, the other (PP-4) crashing in the UK, fortunately while engaged on a high-altitude sortie from which the crew parachuted to safety.

By 1990 much of the development programme was either complete or well in hand, and discussions were in place to decide upon a prime contractor for the Royal Navy's aircraft. It was a condition that the prime contractor must have sufficient financial resources to underwrite any shortfall in compliance, and even the combined resources of Agusta and Westland could not meet this condition.

There followed a competitive process to decide the issue and after some protracted discussions the contract was awarded to IBM (subsequently Loral and finally Lockheed-Martin. The production order for 44 Merlin HM Mk 1s was eventually placed in 1992.

Agusta had taken the lead in the development of the utility (transport) variant, with its rear-loading ramp, and two of the preproduction aircraft (PP-7 and PP-9) were built to this standard.

By the early 1990s Westland were working hard to cultivate interest from the RAF for Merlin (as it was now named) to satisfy a requirement for a medium-lift, high-performance helicopter. In late 1994 an order for twenty-two aircraft was placed.

By this time Westland was part of the GKN group, whilst Agusta had been strengthened by becoming part of Finmecchanica.

The result of this was that EHI could now successfully bid for prime contractorship.

Reliability and maintainability has always been an important part of the EH-101 specification, with severe cost penalties against any shortfall. An important part of the programme was the inclusion of maturity trials, which were undertaken during 1998–2000. Two aircraft (PP-8 and PP-9) were subjected to intensive flying, initially in southern Italy and later in northern Scotland. The two aircraft accumulated more than 2,000 hours each.

The full civil potential of the EH-101 has yet to be realised. Two civil machines have been delivered to Japan, and PP-8 has gained limited certification to demonstrate the very high standard of passenger comfort achievable in this new generation helicopter.

The export potential of the EH-101 is now being realised. After a false start in Canada in 1993, the Cormorant was ordered to meet the tough Canadian Search and Rescue requirement. Production Cormorants are delivered direct from Italy by self-ferry across the Atlantic. Orders have also been confirmed from Denmark and Portugal.

Finally, in 2001 the two companies came together in a joint venture to form AgustaWestland, a major player in the rotorcraft business to become one of the largest helicopter companies in the world.

22 Exocet

Jim Schofield

It took very little time for the military to appreciate that the potential for aviation to be used as a weapon was enormous. The destructive capability of the armed helicopter is witness to what we do with our talents.

Jim Schofield was Weapons Systems Designer, and describes the nature of his work in his book, Developing British Military Helicopters.

Exocet AM 39

Before I went to Pakistan, the Indians had attacked Karachi using Komar fast patrol boats armed with Styx missiles. The missiles had been fired from out at sea and at the time the Pakistan defences had no idea where the missiles had come from. They had caused considerable damage to the naval base and to the oil storage depot where the majority of Pakistan's oil was stored. Pakistan had to have a way to counter this threat. The Exocet AM 39 missile carried on a helicopter was ideal for this purpose. It was very flexible and did not require major support facilities. We entered into detailed discussions with the Navy and with the Aerospatiale team who were in Islamabad.

The missile was to be fitted on to six Westland Sea Kings that had already been delivered to Pakistan. Because the largest part of the contract was for the missiles and its system rather than the installation work, Westland refused to become the prime contractor. Aerospatiale would have to be prime contractor with Westland as the sub-contractor. The Pakistan Navy would have preferred Westland to be Prime Contractor.

The development programme called for a successful missile firing by Aerospatiale/ Westland in France and a second firing in Pakistan by a Navy crew. It was a risky programme because at the time such a large missile had never been fired from a helicopter. The contract discussions were difficult because we had to consider the company liabilities if a firing were not successful. Each missile cost about £1 million.

After three days of discussion we had come to a reasonable agreement with both the Pakistan Navy and with Aerospatiale. The cost was split into a lump sum for development and a cost for the modification of each aircraft. The contract called for stage payment after each section of the work was complete.

The rate of inflation in the UK at the time was over 10 per cent and we were asked if we had taken this into account. The Westland lawyer replied that he had expected the rate to fall shortly and that he had used a much lower rate.

On the final day of discussion Pakistan announced that there would be no stage payments and all monies would be paid on signature of the contract but that the amount would be reduced by the value of inflation that we had assumed. They also announced that they wanted to convert five helicopters rather than the six as originally proposed. The reason for these decisions we discovered was that Pakistan had been given a lump sum by Saudi Arabia to cover the programme. This sum would only cover the modification of five helicopters. Saudi Arabia had also specified that the money must be spent during the current financial year.

The Aerospatiale sale negotiator did not understand what was happening and would not agree to the reduction to five instead of six helicopters. We had to return to a hotel room with a bottle of duty free whisky and explain the reason for the change. It was pointless trying to get more money for the contract and if he did not agree within the next few days, in the financial year, there would be no contract.

I immediately flew home and the following morning reported what had happened and that the programme would require a major engineering commitment. The company had never expected that such a large contract would be signed almost out of the blue after only four days of negotiation. The company's bank overdraft was large and such a major down payment was something that could not be refused. I was one of the few people that realised the risk that we were taking. I sent a coded message to our lawyer and he handed over the contract which I had signed before leaving Pakistan.

Before the contract was signed, I had spent a lot of time with Aerospatiale going through the design and development programme. This was essential in order to obtain a detailed breakdown of the work involved, how long it would take and the cost.

The avionics of the interface between the helicopter and the missile system was relatively simple. The missile required two analogue signals from the helicopter radar to tell it the range and bearing of the target from the helicopter. There was a pointer on the radar display and by fitting a potentiometer, for the range signal, and a synchro, for the bearing signal, to the operator's dials these signal could be supplied directly to the missile.

The two missiles were mounted on beams on each side of the helicopter. The missile had to be fitted between the side of the helicopter and the sponsons which contained the undercarriage.

The support structure for these beams required modification and strengthening to the bathtub and floor of the helicopters. The attachment of the beams to the struc- · ture was through spring struts, and by altering the stiffness of these struts we were able to change the natural frequency of the mounting and avoid any resonance with the helicopter rotor forcing frequencies. We had done the scheme drawings for the installation at Yeovil. When the contract was signed, the detailed design work was transferred to the drawing office at Weston-super-Mare.

The release unit which was designed and manufactured by Aerospatiale was operated by a small explosive charge. This charge pushed a piston which operated a linkage. The linkage pushed the missile forward and then two arms pushed the missile down and away from the helicopter. It was essential that when the rocket motor of the missile fired, one second after the missile was released, that the missile was horizontal and well clear of the helicopter. By adjusting the linkage, the push given by the arms was altered and attitude of the missile at light-up adjusted. If any fault in the system caused the missile to light up near or on the helicopter or at the wrong attitude, the result could have been disaster. We therefore undertook a major failure analysis of the system and carried out numerous rig and flight tests with dummy missiles to ensure that the system was safe. At every stage we made sure that only a double failure could give rise to a problem and that any single failure would be easily detected before or during flight.

The first series of tests were undertaken on a rig in France where large weights were released from prototype release units. We then did a series of releases of dummy missiles from a helicopter at Salisbury Plain. These missiles had the same weight, centre of gravity position and geometry as the live missiles. We had to do releases with a number of different flight conditions, including the safe release and jettison of both missiles with the helicopter in an autorotative descent that would follow a complete engine failure. When the missiles left the helicopter they slowly rotated into a nose-down position, like a dart, and finished up embedded 6ft into the earth.

During tests Aerospatiale had discovered that the missile did not achieve the predicted and contracted range. The missile was flying at too high an incidence and most of the lift was generated from the missile body rather than the wings. This resulted in increased drag and hence reduced range. To reduce the incidence, larger wings were required. Because the missile was installed on the Sea King between the fuselage and the sponsons, the wing size was restricted. We made a number of plywood wings and tried them on the aircraft. We eventually came up with a trapezoidal shape which we flew with plasticine stuck on the wing tips to determine the clearance from the fuselage and sponson skins.

The live firing of the missiles was to be undertaken in France. We had a meeting at Yeovil to discuss the firing programme. I chaired the meeting and was surprised to find that the Aerospatiale representatives included their Chief Engineer and Chief Development Engineer as well as the normal member of their team with whom we had been dealing. The Westland test pilot 'Tom' Bowler and the flight test crew who had done the drop trials were present. The meeting went well until we came to the makeup of the trials team when the Aerospatiale Chief Development Engineer said that it was essential for safety reasons that the pilot should be fluent in French! Tom replied with a 'Oui, Monsieur'. His next question, which got the same reply from Tom, was that the pilot must be fully *au fait* with the French range procedures and must therefore be a graduate of the French Test Pilots School at Bretigny. The French have insisted that anything important that they have a part in must be seen to be led by a Frenchman. The test pilot on the first Concorde flight, the engine driver on the first train through the Channel Tunnel or more recently the pilot on the first flight of the A380 were all Frenchmen.

The French Development Engineer then shouted at Tom in rapid French to which Tom replied equally fluently before getting up and leaving the meeting. He returned a few moments later with a framed citation, which he had removed from his office wall. It stated that Tom had graduated as a qualified test pilot at the French Test Pilots School. There was an exchange scheme where the British Services would send one of their pilots to the French school and the French would send a pilot to the British school at Boscombe Down. Tom had been such an exchange pilot.

Aerospatiale continued to try to have their pilot conduct the firing trial but the Commandant of the French Test Pilots School wrote them a letter stating that all the pilots who graduated from his school were trained to the same very high standard and that to suggest otherwise was a slight on his organisation.

The firing took place from the Isle de Levant, an island off the south coast of France near Frezus. About 90 per cent of the Isle de Levant was owned by the French Government and used as a testing base. The remaining 10 per cent was a nudist colony.

We flew the aircraft down to the South of France. There was some difficulty with the aircraft registration. In the UK it had a civil registration; as it crossed the Channel it should have reverted to a Pakistan registration and then when carrying the missiles it needed a French Military registration.

During the week we stayed on the island but at the weekend we flew back to a French air base near Cannes and stayed in a hotel. While flying back near Frejus we saw the result of a disaster that happened in the 1940s. A dam had broken and the resulting torrent caused an enormous amount of damage and killed many hundreds of people. Because it happened at the end of the Second World War the disaster was not publicised. During the weekend, Tom and I walked up to the site of the dam and found that blocks of concrete the size of very large houses had been carried over five miles down stream by the water. It made one feel very small.

Because of the large amount of shipping in the area, the missiles were fitted with reduced-size rocket motors to reduce their range. We got up at three in the morning to be ready for a firing at first light but sea mists, large amounts of shipping and a Russian spy trawler often caused the trial to be aborted. It took over three weeks before we completed the two firings. One problem that Aerospatiale encountered was an interference between the radio altimeter on the missile and the radio altimeters on the Sea King and the chase helicopter. The missile picked up the signal from the helicopters and dived towards the sea. The altimeter aperture on the missile had to be closed up to overcome this problem.

The firings were successful, allowing modified helicopters to be delivered to the customer.

The Pakistan Navy carried out a firing themselves, selecting a missile, with a live warhead, at random from their supply. They fired against an old British Second World War minesweeper and completely removed the whole of the ship's superstructure.

The Exocet installation was a large engineering task. Because Westland was modifying helicopters that they had already sold to Pakistan it did not directly bring into the factory any new helicopter manufacture. The Exocet did, though, bring in a very large order from India. The Indians now required a weapon to counter the Pakistan Sea Kings and they bought a large number of Sea Kings fitted with the British Aerospace Sea Eagle Missile.

23 Airborne Early Warning

Jim Schofield

It is a well-established fact that the radar chain around the south coast was one of the major contributory factors in the successful outcome of the 'Battle of Britain'.

The war in the Pacific, which was waged between two carrier battle fleets, emphasised the need for maritime forces to carry their own Airborne Early Warning (AEW) capability.

By the early 1950s, the US Navy had carrier-borne aircraft equipped with powerful radar for this role. The Royal Navy acquired and operated American-built Douglas AD-4W Skyraiders in 1953 to carry out the AEW role until the Fairey Gannet AEW Mk 3 replaced them.

When Westland acquired the Fairey Aviation Company's commitments in 1960, they became responsible for the continued support for the Gannet, even though by this time Westland was essentially a rotorcraft company.

Thus it was that for some fifteen years after declaring themselves a helicopter company Westland was still involved in fixed-wing operations. However, what this did do was to establish an expertise in the avionics aspects of AEW that came to the fore dramatically in the 1980s.

The Gannets never operated out of Yeovil, but the workforce and airfield residents were treated to the occasional flypast from these big machines, which represented the last fixed-wing aircraft involving Westland technicians and aircrew.

The last Gannet flew out of Weston-super-Mare in February 1976, marking the end of sixty years of fixed-wing activity by Westland.

In 1978 a political decision was made that, in order to reduce costs, the Gannet programme should be scrapped and that the Royal Air Force would undertake all the AEW duties using aging Shackletons and the Nimrod Aircraft. The RAF was capable of providing AEW cover over 99 per cent of the world's surface, the remaining 1 per cent being the Falkland Islands!

And where did the need for AEW arise? Jim Schofield explains what happened.

When I first took up my post as Weapons Designer at Yeovil, one of my first tasks was to produce a project study for an AEW version of the Wessex helicopter. As new radars were produced and the Sea King came into service, we updated this study and submitted the studies to MOD. In response we normally received a telephone call from the RN desk officer wishing that the Navy could be allowed to have it. On one occasion it landed on the desk of an RAF officer and we received a very strongly worded reply informing us that the RAF were capable of doing the complete AEW role and it was not up to a private MOD contractor to try and alter government policy.

When HMS *Sheffield* was sunk by an Exocet AM 39 missile fired from a Super Étendard aircraft the need for AEW cover for the fleet became critical. I was summonsed with the Sea King Project Manager, Rollie Fish, to an afternoon meeting at MOD PE on Thursday 13 May and warned that the MOD had booked a hotel for us as they expected the meeting to continue through to the next day.

The meeting consisted of representatives from the Royal Navy, the Sea King Project Office, the Radar Branch, Thorn EMI and Westland. The radar people tabled a sketch of a Thorn EMI Searchwater radar with retractable radar on the side of the Sea King and I was asked if it could be done. The sketch was very close to the project study we had done a year or so before and I replied in the affirmative. The next question from the Navy was could it be done in three months so that the helicopters could join the replacement fleet that was being assembled at that time. Again I replied in the affirmative.

A large percentage of the workforce at Westland had relatives – husbands, sons and friends on the Task Force – and the support for the Navy was enormous. I realised this when I phoned up the store department at the start of the crisis and asked if they had any weapon-mounting lugs. Normally the response would have been 'Have you got a part number?', 'What's the order number?', 'I'll have a look when I've time and you'll have to get a request signed by the MOD RTO (Resident Technical Office)'. In this case the response was 'I'll let you know, Sir' and about twenty minutes later the store man appeared at my office and deposited ten lugs on my desk with a promise to get the remaining lugs by the following morning. This attitude continued throughout the Falklands War and it was a joy to work in such an environment. I don't think I ever had to tell anybody twice to do something. Without this attitude it would have been impossible to complete the aircraft in three months.

When I went in to work on Friday morning the great majority of my colleagues were very supportive and agreed that we could do it. There were a few people, mainly those in their 40s who were afraid that a failure might affect their chances of promotion, who did not want anything to do with the project. One of these was my immediate boss who thought I had gone mad. While my boss did not take part in the project, he did not in any way stop me trying to do it, for which I was grateful. The Nimrod AEW aircraft with the Searchwater radar had been in development for a number of years, it was late, over budget and still not working. I had agreed to do the same job in three months.

The Divisional Technical Director, Alan Doe, came into my office on Friday morning and said I could have anyone in the technical department to work on the Sea King. I replied that I wanted the best aerodynamicist in the company. Alan had been Chief Aerodynamicist before being promoted and I said I wanted him to do the aerodynamics. He took a GA (general arrangement) drawing of the helicopter and departed in the direction of the wind tunnel. He returned on Saturday with a full set of wind tunnel results including stability derivatives. From these results we were able to calculate the performance of the helicopter, estimate the loads on the radome and forces required to raise and lower it and also determine the stability of the machine.

When the aircraft flight data became available, his predictions of the helicopter performance were proved to be very accurate.

I had agreed that Westland would produce a full project report by Monday morning. Each section of the company that would be involved in the aircraft produced a section of the report, Project Management, Avionics, Weights, Structures, Service Department etc. and we put these together on Sunday afternoon. The programme started with required date into service and then we slotted all the other activities into the time available. Not the way one normally produces a design and development programme. It seemed just about feasible.

On Sunday the secretaries had the help of a Naval Commander in reading the report and correcting any errors and then copying and stapling the report together. As soon as the report was complete the Commander took it up to London.

As Chief Designer (Defensive Systems) I would not normally have been responsible for the design of a new mark of aircraft unless it involved major Weapons or Survivability features and it was the MOD and Navy who decided that I should be the Designer-in-Charge of the AEW Sea King. There were two reasons for this. Firstly, the work we had done fitting weapons to the helicopters had gone very well and we had a team from design, manufacturing, development and flight test that had worked very well together and MOD did not want to set up a second team which could involve a clash of priorities.

Secondly, there was the Old Boy network; I had always worked well with the Navy and Ministry Officials right back to my National Service days and people who I had served with in the Navy were now senior officers in the Navy. Mike Simpson, who had replaced me as Assistant Air Engineering Officer (AEO) on 845 Squadron just prior to the Suez Invasion was now Controller (Air) and David Halifax who was TAS Office was now the Admiral mainly responsible for putting the task force together. Mike and I were both aware that when one is preparing to go to war, it does focus the mind on the important issues that need to be solved quickly. Some years before, it was thought that the IRA had acquired some SA-7 anti-aircraft missiles and he rushed down to see me at Westland, and with Pete Brammer (the engine installation designer at Westland) we produced an infrared suppression unit for the Army Lynx helicopters which went into service in about a month.

Requirement and Specification

The Navy made the decision to proceed with the AEW Sea King immediately and the Captain DNAW (Director Naval Air Warfare) Ben Bathurst (later First Sea Lord) came down to Yeovil and we sat either side of the table in my office; he wrote the aircraft requirement while I calculated from the wind tunnel results if it could be achieved.

The requirement was very simple and covered just one and a half pages of A4. Two Sea Kings were to be able to provide twenty-four-hour cover seven days a week at 100nm in front of the task force at a height of 10,000ft. After each sortie a time of one hour was to be allowed for refuelling, crew change and maintenance. The two aircraft were to be in service within three months.

We repeated the calculations a number of times and agreed a compromise which I thought that Westland could achieve and which met the Royal Navy's basic needs. The problem that the Navy had was that while the down time was sufficient for Before Flight and Daily Inspections there was insufficient time for the longer inspections. Ben looked at a number of options to overcome the problem including splitting the inspections so that each time an aircraft was on the deck, part of the inspection was undertaken. He also looked at providing an airborne Harrier screen when there was no AEW cover and flying the Sea Kings from a ship in front of the Task Force so reducing the transit time.

We agreed and signed the contract that day: Nat Mills from Project Management and I signed for Westlands. Whether we should have signed such a large contract without reference to higher authority was debateable. In our minds there was no alternative; the Navy needed the AEW Sea King. If we had refused to sign, the Navy would probably have never placed a contract with Westland again, and finally the contract was a 'cost plus contract' with Westland being paid at the highest MOD rate.

Because the aircraft were complete and in-service within the three months the MOD also got a very good deal because when the aircraft were delivered all work and bookings on the contract at Westland stopped. Most overspends on MOD contracts result from overruns which often continue for years. There followed a very frustrating ten days. The two Searchwater radar sets that we needed were spares for the Nimrod AEW programme and the Royal Air Force refused to release them to the Navy. I had arranged with Stan Griggs, who was in charge of the Westland drawing office at Weston-super-Mare, that most of the design work would be done at Weston. Stan had been the Designer-in-Charge of the Gannet Mk 3 AEW aircraft at Fairey Aviation at Hayes before we were taken over by Westlands. For ten days we remained in limbo.

Security

With every MOD contract there is a 'secret letter' which defines the level of secrecy for each part of the work. The secret letter for the AEW Sea King was bigger than the main contract.

The Navy were concerned that we could not complete the aircraft in time for them to join the Replacement Task Force and that if this happened the Argentineans would know that the Task Force had no AEW cover. They classified the whole project as SECRET.

I was very concerned that almost none of my superiors could stop or at least delay the project and if we had to attend all the meetings and discussions that normally went with such a project it would delay the work for weeks. Capt. Bathurst said that the solution was simple; the project would be classified as top secret on a need-to-know basis and that only those people who were working directly on the project could be involved. If anyone did anything to delay the project I was to inform either him or the MOD Resident Technical Officer immediately and that person would be warned off and, if necessary, would lose their security clearance and be escorted from the factory or arrested under the official secrets act. We never had to take that drastic step although on one occasion John Firmin, the Head of Avionics, got a memo from his boss ordering him to stop certain work but John's secretary misfiled the memo until after the work was complete.

I never believed such a security system would ever work and that everybody in the company would be aware of what we were doing. It did work rather better than we anticipated.

On the Sunday just before we were preparing the first aircraft for flight, I opened the *Sunday Times* and found a large article with a very bad drawing by their defence correspondent on the AEW Sea King. It reported an interview with a Westland director stating that such an aircraft could be built and in service within nine months if the MOD would only make a decision. I had been away on the previous Friday and the director had phoned my office and asked for the unclassified project note that I had written a year or so before. One of the draughtsmen had gone to see the director with a General Arrangement drawing of the helicopter but beat a very hasty retreat when he found that the director knew nothing of the project and that the man with him was a reporter.

On Monday morning I went into the flight hangar very early and at 8.30 a.m. my secretary phoned up to say that there were some gentlemen to see me and could I return to my office immediately. There were two police cars parked outside the drawing office block and a uniformed policeman guarding the main door. I found anther policeman outside my office door. As I entered my office the Westland security officer produced a copy of the paper and asked me if I knew how the report had appeared in the paper.

When I said I did know, one of the other gentlemen jumped forward. 'I am a police superintendent. I am investigating a very serious breach of security and I must caution you that anything you say may be used in evidence against you' etc. My immediate reaction was 'What a damn fine way to start a Monday morning.' I tried to explain that there had been no breach of security and that article had appeared because our security was very good. The policemen, who must have left London about 5 o'clock in the morning, were determined to arrest someone, and could not believe that a director whose office was only 50 yards down the corridor from the drawing office and whose windows overlooked the flight hangar could have no idea what we were doing.

We all trooped down the corridor where, being Monday morning, the director was holding a divisional meeting with all his heads of department. The arrival of the uniformed police brought the meeting to an abrupt end and it then took a very long time to convince the policemen what had happened and that they had made a wasted journey to Yeovil.

Technical Problems

One thing that concerned me initially was the radome. It was a flexible bag of Kevlar and when the radar was switched on it was pressurised by a small pump to 4in of water pressure. It worked very well and I was told that the distortion to the radar signal was much less than that for a rigid radome.

There were two main areas of technical concern. The first was the centre of gravity of the helicopter. In order to achieve the maximum time on station we needed to carry full fuel and this required getting the helicopter centre of gravity correct. Every morning the weight engineer, Mrs Pat Marsden, would prepare a weight statement based on the design data or on the weight of components as they were produced. It became clear that the centre of gravity was not right and we had to move a group of avionic boxes to correct it. The C of G was still very critical and even with the best weight distribution, at take-off with full fuel, the Observer/Co-pilot needed to remain in the co-pilot's seat. To remain within the C of G limits, he should not go back into the main cabin until the aircraft had burnt off fuel and reached cruising conditions. The Radar Rating would switch on and set up the Searchwater radar during the climb.

The radome raise and lower system would not normally have presented a problem but because of the very short time scale it was not possible to type test and certify any major changes to the hydraulic system. There were three hydraulic systems on the Sea King. Two primary systems operated the flight controls and any alteration to these systems would entail a major test and approval work. We decided to use only the third hydraulic system which operated the auxiliary units such as the rescue winch.

It was necessary to use an approved jack, and after much searching through the Westland store we acquired three jacks that were suitable. They were flight control jacks for the Wessex. We had estimated the loads on the radome from the wind tunnel measurements and had no accurate figure for the jack load. I would have liked to have fitted a larger jack in case our figures were too low but there was no suitable jack available.

Because we only had a single hydraulic supply we needed a way to raise the radome in an emergency and we fitted a hand pump with its own small reservoir and changeover valve.

The development people built a test rig to test the whole system but the test rig, rather than the actual system, kept on breaking. As we didn't have any failures of the actual system we assumed it would work OK.

Hydraulic System Diagrams

The raise and lower was operated by the radar operator by a switch. The hand-operated emergency pump was situated at the back of the cabin behind the firewall. When one cranked the handle a small valve moved to cut off the supply from the pump and then fed oil to the jack to raise the radome. It took about eight minutes pumping to raise the radome. The system worked well and we had no problems with the system on the first two aircraft.

As a precaution against an aircraft being unable to land because the radome was stuck down I had a pit dug at the side of the airfield so that the aircraft could land with its wheels on the airfield and the dome down the hole. The pilots were not happy with this as it meant that they might have to make a tricky landing.

After I had left the programme, about a year later, the Navy ordered more AEW Sea Kings and on the first test flight of one of these aircraft they were unable to raise the radome. The aircraft flew back to the airfield to land over the hole. During the intervening period the Health and Safety men, bless them, had found the hole and concreted in the sides and put iron railing round it. As the aircraft flew round the airfield the Westland Fire Brigade set to with their cutters to remove the railings. Before landing, the crew operated the raise switch and the system operated normally and the radome came up.

The crew were new to the aircraft and during the flight the operator had found the hand pump and cranked it, shutting off the main hydraulic supply. If he had known how the system worked, he could have raised the dome by continuing to pump. As the aircraft circled the airfield the oil had slowly seeped past the valve and the spring moved the valve back to the normal position.

My boss was very annoyed by the incident and wanted to blame me but I responded that he should get his flight test engineers to read the aircraft operating notes before they flew in a new helicopter.

The heat generated by such a large amount of high-powered electronic equipment in the cabin was considerable and we had to install a fan to draw cooling through the cabin. Initially, the fan produced more noise than the helicopter when it took off. We had to install larger ducts.

Avionic System

At the start of the programme a decision had been made that no alterations should be made to optimise the Searchwater radar. The radar software was extremely complex and any alteration could spell disaster. The radar was optimised for the Nimrod aircraft for operation at about 25,000ft. The Sea King maximum altitude was only 10,000ft and some of the equipment such as pumps etc. was only cleared for that altitude. A test programme was put in hand and the aircraft was later cleared for 12,000ft.

Capt. Bathurst's main objective was to get AEW cover for the fleet and he told me to tell him if any of his staff asked for any equipment to be fitted to the helicopters which might delay its entry into service. I was surprised to find as I walked round the helicopters that they were being modified and that a large number of aerials and other bits of equipment seemed to be bolted on to the fuselages, and little groups of people from various electrical firms were working in the factory.

I found out that the naval staffs had asked if we could fit a radar warning receiver (which warned the crew if someone was watching them on radar) and various other communication equipment (such as IFF Interrogation Friend or Foe). As I was assured that this work would not delay the helicopter programme I took no action and to this day I have no idea what was finally fitted to the helicopters.

On the Crane

In order to test the radar on the ground it was necessary to lift the helicopter so that the radome could be lowered. I suggested that we should build a wooden ramp and push the helicopter up on to it. The development people said that they would lift the helicopter on a crane. I agreed provided we didn't finish up with the helicopter hanging on the crane while they tried to find the operator. The security officer then phoned me up to say that he had a crane driver at the main gate wanting to enter the airfield for some secret project. The man had no security clearance. I looked out of my office window and saw a massive crane blocking the entrance to the factory and I told the security officer that he needed to be cleared very quickly and after a few questions to ensure that he didn't have an Argentinean grandmother they let him in.

The Thorn EMI team had spent the whole of the day trying to get the radar working in the hangar and by about 9 o'clock in the evening it was clear that they were very tired and I told them that it was essential that we checked out the hydraulic system and they would have to stop work for the day. As we connected up the tractor and pulled the helicopter out of the hangar at about 11 p.m. everybody stopped work and clapped and cheered. The hangar cleaners immediately started cleaning the hangar of the results of a month's hard work and within about two hours had it looking spotless, with all the tools and rigs cleaned and ready for further use.

Because of the secrecy of the project, Yeovil Police patrolled the local roads and cleared off the courting couples who used the little road that ran beside the airfield.

The hydraulic system worked perfectly and after raising and lowering the radome using a hydraulic rig a few times and pumping it to the up position manually, we lowered the helicopter from the crane and returned it to the hangar.

In the morning when the Thorn EMI team returned they started to clear the radar system again and this time everything worked. They had been working for the last month twelve hours a day, seven days a week.

We hung the helicopter on the crane and started operating the radar. It was a very powerful radar and a major concern was whether the radar emissions would affect the helicopter electronic systems. Normally, Westland would undertake their compatibility trials and then the helicopter would go to Boscombe Down for the Ministry to undertake their own trials. To save time both sets of test were done together and the Boscombe Down experts came to Yeovil and did their tests when they could be fitted in between the aircraft clearance tests. These tests were completed in the early hours of the morning and I remarked that now we needed to find the crane operator to lower the aircraft. The Development Engineer banged on the door of the cab and a very sleepy crane driver appeared. He had been living in the cab for the last few days.

There is a clearly defined procedure, in Air Publication AP 970, which must be completed before any Service aircraft can be flown. Each specialist designer, such as Aerodynamics, Weights, Structures and Avionics, has to sign a check sheet to certify that their particular area meets all the relevant safety requirements. Finally the Chief Designer signs the aircraft off for flight. The Chief Designer, who had handed in his notice and was leaving the company, had taken no part in the design of the AEW Sea King and I knew that we would have difficulty in getting him to sign the clearance form. His deputy was the man who had told me I was mad and wanted no part in the project.

The Airworthiness Engineer brought me the check form, which all the specialist designers had signed, and I signed the list as Chief Designer (Defensive Systems). He then produced the main clearance form and I found that I was named The Westland Chief Designer. The Ministry of Defence had anticipated the problem. Legally, the Chief Designer had to be a Chief Designer of the company who had been approved by the MOD. Attached to the form was a letter from the Controller Air in the MOD specifying that I, as a Chief Designer, had been approved as the Company Chief

Designer with authority to sign off aircraft for flight. The Controller Air at MOD was Mike Simpson, who I had served with on 845 Squadron during my National Service twenty-five years before. A couple of days later the original Westland nominee for the post of Chief Designer was approved by MOD. I suspect that I was the shortest serving Chief Designer ever.

We flew the aircraft early the following morning. There is less turbulence early in the morning and there were fewer people around to watch. We lowered and raised the radome and checked the aircraft flight characteristics. All was as predicted and we were then able to start testing the radar and avionic equipment. Even at 10,000ft the performance of the radar was exceptional.

As soon as the Royal Navy knew that the aircraft and radar system worked they immediately relaxed the security and declassified the fact that they now had an AEW helicopter. A few days later they demonstrated the helicopters to the public at the Yeovilton Air Day.

The AEW Sea Kings have been in service for over twenty-five years and the helicopters have recently been completely refurbished and updated so that they can remain in service for a further fifteen years. Not a bad achievement for a helicopter which was expected to be in service for just two years.

The Falkland Islands had been recaptured and the war was over before the AEW Sea Kings were deployed in the area but they still played an important part in maintaining the peace. At the start of the war, the Argentinean cruiser *General Belgrano* had been torpedoed with a large loss of life, and the Argentinean Navy wanted revenge. They still had Super Étendard aircraft and possibly Exocet missiles and the Royal Navy was very concerned that they would make a surprise attack and sink the British carriers.

24 Going for a Song

David Gibbings

An ability to paint is regarded by most of us as a talent to be valued. David Gibbings, when he arrived at Yeovil, found himself fully engrossed in house hunting and with time on his hands.

He decided to revive an old spark of interest that had always been with him: a wish to paint. He enrolled in the local art college, and quickly developed into a competent aviation artist; since that time he has, in fact, produced over 200 paintings that are now spread all over the world.

Many have a tale to tell, none more so than this one.

My wife Mary maintained a small sheep farm in the village of Odcombe just outside Yeovil, on the approach to the airfield. Every spring we had a number of regular visitors, when our friends brought their children to see the lambs.

This was always a happy time, full of activity and there were always a few lambs which required bottle feeding. The place was filled with the sound of children, bleating lambs and mothers, both ovine and human, trying without a hope of success to control their offspring.

The spring of 1982 was no exception. For several years I had been totally engrossed with helicopter icing trials, a task that had entailed spending whole winters away in Denmark and Canada 'looking for trouble' in the form of icing, while trying to develop a rotor blade de-icing system for the EH-101 (Merlin).

Such trials were mounted as joint exercises by the MOD and the Contractor (Westland), and as such were closely monitored by the Project Office in London, in this case, working with a serving Commander in the Royal Navy. I was fortunate in having to work with Chris, a hands-on engineer who understood the complexity of the business and the stress this could put upon those trying to make it all work. We had become firm friends, and his family had become one of our regular visitors.

Chris had just relinquished his job in the Project Office, and was destined for Staff College, and, I certainly had no doubt, greater things. He and I set off on our part of the ritual, to walk the bounds, chatting freely, setting the world to rights in the process.

There was plenty to talk about. In the Southern Ocean the Argentinean' forces had occupied the Falkland Islands and other British outposts. The news was full of speculation as Britain, caught completely on the wrong foot, attempted to mobilise a task force from what was available after a decade of a somewhat confused defence policy.

I asked Chris whether he was likely to be involved and received an emphatic No; he would have to watch it all going on from the Staff College.

Two nights later the call came; 'Report to "Norland" immediately.' Apparently H. Jones had arrived at the dockside with his boys and with his unique approach to protocol had quickly found himself at odds with the captain, who was no shrinking violet. The two met head-on and it was clear that their relationship would not help with the job in hand.

Chris, as a serving RN officer, was tasked with coming between these two to calm things down.

The Task Force sailed. Each ship had been loaded hastily and requiring redistribution and documentation, in many cases things had ended up on the wrong ship. As the fleet sailed south, helicopters plied from one to the other transforming order from chaos. Indeed it was the helicopters that made the whole exercise possible; over two hundred aircraft were taken south and they were in use all the way down. They had all been built at Yeovil and without them, success would have been unlikely.

Chris's wife came to see us on a few occasions, and on one brought several letters which had arrived together; they started with 'Ha ha, this is a laugh, it'll all be over before we get there.' Then Ascension Island, 'Hey, it's all beginning to get a bit serious.' Finishing up with San Carlos sound, and the serious reality of war in the raw.

Chris served with distinction in the Falklands campaign, and deservedly was appropriately decorated.

A few years after the Falklands, Westland ran into hard times. The UK military orders expected to revive our capability were nowhere near as large as had been hoped, and the Westland civil project, the Westland 30, had run into problems operating in the USA, and was not faring well in the world markets. The company had to generate enough financial strength to continue trading, and without new aircraft coming off the line would need to find a strong financial partner. This was the essence of the 'Westland Affair'.

As an artist, I was sufficiently moved by the situation to produce a painting; it depicted two Sea Kings, with the task force, all against the background of San Carlos sound, I placed Norland in a prominent place as a personal tribute to my friend.

The painting, which measured 36 x 21in (54 x 91cm) was produced from the outset as a tribute to Yeovil's contribution to the Falklands campaign. The message was clear: 'We played our part in the nation's hour of need.' We could do with some help now. The chosen title was '… and they all came up from Somerset'.

The title was taken from a song written at the time of William and Mary, 'We've all come up from Somerset, where the cider apples grow …', and tells of a Somerset family on a day out in London, where they meet the king, as one is likely to, of course. The farmer husband sings of the strength and skill of Somerset yeomen, and the wife extols the virtues and beauty of Somerset maids.

The young son explains that he wants to be a soldier by singing:

And if it's soldier boys you need, and it's fighting for to do.
Just send the word to Somerset, and we'll all come up for you.

I placed the finished work in the nearby Fleet Air Arm Museum, where it was hung in a prestigious position in the main lecture theatre; before doing so I arranged for about 1,000 prints to be made by our local paper, the *Western Gazette*. These would be offered for sale in aid of a service charity.

It had not been on show for long before I received a call from the museum to the effect that an American visitor had expressed an interest in buying it, offering a princely sum (at least for me) of $1,000 plus shipping. At that time this was probably the highest price I had ever been offered for a single work. Shortly afterwards I received a telephone call from a Mr Stuart Lee Adelman PhD, who was attached to the US Navy as an education officer, and who was serving at sea, and was currently transferring to a new ship. I took him at his word and proceeded to pack and ship his picture. The handsome cheque arrived, accompanied with a letter extolling the virtues of the painting and my own skill. I wasted no time paying the cheque into my account. After several weeks the cheque reappeared liberally annotated with all the indications that it had 'bounced', and my calls to all known addresses failed to raise him.

The shipping firm had the same problem; my worst fears were justified. Mr Adelman had disappeared without trace.

And so I resigned myself to the loss, although, having gone to print I did in fact do remarkably well.

Twenty-five years later

I occasionally check out the Internet for mention of my work. You can imagine my surprise when there before my eyes was my original painting, for sale on eBay!

The vendor was not, of course, Mr Adelman, but a respected gallery that had acquired it legitimately at a public sale. Naturally I contacted them, but they had already sold the work on to a client in Ohio.

I wrote to the buyer, explaining that I had no intention of reclaiming the painting. After all, he had purchased it honestly and seemed well pleased with what he had, but I did feel that he would be interested in the provenance of 'his' painting.

It turned out that he was an expat from Taunton, and, needless to say, I had made a friend.

When he visited his parents some time later, he came to see me and we raised a glass to an interesting story and confusion to Mr Adelman's endeavours.

But that is not quite the end of the story. Sometime later, his mother called me to tell me that his grandfather had died and that she wanted to get him something to remember him by. The result was that she bought one of my paintings, and with the proceeds, I in turn acquired a small laptop computer, something that has helped me immensely with my lecturing activities.

I am not sure that this tale adds much to the Westland story, but it does give a glimpse at what goes on in a quiet country town, and perhaps that what goes around, comes around. As regards Mr Adelman, I am sure that most of his associates were of a similar mind to himself – enjoy their company; you deserve each other.

25 Ode to the Wessex

David Baston

After the Second World War, Westland made the decision to concentrate future activity on helicopters, and to do so established the agreement to produce Sikorsky designs under licence.

This approach has been the subject of much debate, but did in fact serve Westland well, placing them in a position of strength when the industry was 'rationalised' in the 1960s, such that they were able to take the lead as 'Westland Helicopters'.

It must not be assumed that the Westland-built versions were direct copies; all the Sikorsky-designed machines were extensively re-worked and universally acclaimed by the users.

The Wessex was a good example. Modified to accept gas turbines and, with a sophisticated auto-pilot, it remained in service with the RN and RAF for forty years and was looked upon with a great deal of affection by those who flew it or flew in it. This included several members of the Royal Family.

When the Wessex HU Mk 5 was retired from service in the Royal Navy, the following lament by Lt Cdr David Baston appeared in Cockpit, *the Royal Navy's flight safety magazine, and was subsequently reproduced in John Beattie's book* Fly Navy.

Well, it's gorn – finally and irretrievably gorn. A lovely old helicopter that was already an elderly design when Westlands (those well-known makers of garage doors) got their hands on it and turned a single piston-engined, American design into the twin turbine Wessex 5. The stories surrounding the aircraft are legion and its reputation for being rugged and safe, if not always reliable flying, made it a firm favourite with those of us who were lucky enough to fly it. I suspect that never again will we have a helicopter that has such a superb single-engine performance and such enormous reserves of power when both were running. Some of the torque figures pulled are firmly burned into the minds of those who just kept pulling on the collective lever to avoid impending doom!

There was a well-known Commander (Air) of a Naval Air Station who managed the ultimate in Australia by pulling so much torque that the complete rotor head came off. He must surely hold the record for over-torqueing, though I am sure that as a Helicopter Warfare Instructor (HWI) he wouldn't admit to ever looking at the torque meter, even if he'd known where it was. Luckily, the head came off on take-off, so the dozens of Australians occupying the fourteen available seats came tumbling out of the back, whingeing but unscathed.

Engine-off landings were a fertile area for experiment, and it surely was one of the few helicopters that could be safely 'engined off' without having to use the collective lever. All it took was bags of nerve, even more speed than normal and a certainty that no one important was watching you! The trick was to utilise the flare, quite precisely, to reduce ground speed and rate of descent to arrive with little of both, then roll the tail wheel on early and – the brave and clever bit – tilt the rotor disc rearward as the front end lowered itself to the tarmac. Minor problems were always in the back of the pilot's mind, such as too much rearward tilt and you chopped your own tail off! This made it a spectator sport of some note, with many cries of '*Chicken!*' over the radio to the not so brave, as it was very obvious when someone cheated and used the lever at the last moment! Did I say cheat by using the lever?

Strength at all ends of the machine was always a great bonus. No one who saw the brilliant arrival in dispersal, after an air display rehearsal at Yeovilton, will forget one Squadron Commanding Officer's dashing arrival as he bounced the tailwheel off the top of a ground power unit with a good twenty degrees of nose up, recovered, then landed for the second time in front of his surprised and by now rather nervous marshaller. There were also the chaps in Singapore who returned to dispersal after an Instrument Training trip (supposedly being conducted at several thousand feet) that had a goodly portion of the main telephone cables between Singapore and Kuala Lumpur wrapped neatly round the aircraft's nose and undercarriage! It was bad luck, that one, because they only hit them while avoiding a train …

A particularly good demonstration of the ruggedness of the old girl was also amply displayed on an Instrument Flying (IF) trip in Cornwall. The pilot under test was the Squadron CO, who had the added disability of being a Royal Marine to whom IF and quite lot of other things (like holding a knife and fork) did not come naturally. Well, at the end of the trip the aforesaid RM was actually on centre line and glide-path, so the IRI (Instrument Rating Instructor) decided to let the Jolly Green Giant continue below break-off height under the hood to see what happened!

Well, the JGG just sat and held everything nice and steady, locked onto the instruments, with the result that the aircraft struck the ground a shrewd blow at a steady 90 knots, sticking there as if superglued as the combined team of IRI and RM JGG could not work out what to do next – or even who had control at that stage!

Wings knew what to do, though; he picked up his phone with one hand and watched the aircraft with binos in the other, because if you see the disaster you legally cannot be on the Board of Inquiry! Well, the aircraft passed the tower, slowing only slightly with faint wisps of brake dust beginning to show, and a fairly impressive amount of rearward cyclic finally caused the aircraft to come to a halt halfway down the rather long runway. The subsequent debrief was not entirely dominated by the IRI, as is usual, but Wings certainly had an awful lot to say.

To my certain knowledge it is also the only helicopter ever to have successfully taken on a Sea Harrier in air-to-air combat and won, forcing the damaged 'Stovie' to return to base unable to continue his sortie, whilst the victorious and gallant Wessex 5 crew, of which I was the captain, landed in the car park at a nearby inn and celebrated their historic victory.

This followed a mid-air collision in cloud and resulted in a little cosmetic surgery being required around the tail wheel area of the Wessex plus a new tailfin for the SHAR. Spookily, the Air Traffic Team on watch at the time happened to be husband and wife, one of whom was controlling me and the other Willie MacAtee, a US Marine Corps exchange pilot in the Sea Harrier. More importantly than these key details was the fact that husband and wife had 'withdrawn ambassadors' at the time of the incident – and subsequently divorced!

If the Wessex 5 had a weakness, it was its tendency not to start when it was really necessary. It damned well knew when you were on a VIP trip and would flatly refuse to start, but then after the chap had departed, fuming and late by car, it would start as though nothing had happened! The attitude of 'Command' was always to have a spare for a spare for a spare, especially at long weekends, to ensure the job could be done. The dodgy starting was made worse in later years by the air engineers changing the batteries to smaller ones without telling us operators. This certainly made going home for lunch, or stopping off at a cafe or beauty spot whilst in transit, a much more exciting business!

No one to my knowledge ever got caught out by the powers that be, but several Wessex have been known to fly quite long distances, on one engine, to places where it could then be admitted that the other would not start! It knew when things were really serious, though, and rarely failed on an SAR mission, or on one glorious occasion in the days of short exhaust pipes, when an aircraft in the middle of a line of eighteen others on Salisbury Plain did a wet start and set fire to the grass. The others all started wonderfully that day, thank goodness, and rapidly flew away from the now-raging fire!

When it first went out to Borneo, this tendency not to start, especially when hot, meant that you did not shut down whilst pausing between tasks. However, to reduce fuel consumption and noise it was common to pull the speed selects back to about 200 rotor RPM or less (they would normally be at 230). The interesting bit came when you took off, especially if you forgot to push them back up again. The aircraft would stagger into the air (and if you were lucky down a slope), its rotor blades coning like a ballerina's arms whilst you struggled to get the revs back – without the passengers knowing anything was amiss and, of course, before you struck the trees!

Radios were another interesting quirk of the early Wessex 5.

It had a marvellous HF set that could receive every known commercial radio station from all round the world, plus the ability to talk clearly to Malta from the Culdrose local area. What it could not do, however, was to talk to Culdrose from the local area or any other Naval Air Station from any other area! Whether this was due to the Ops Wrens spending more time on their nails (or perhaps the Ops Chief) than listening to deafening static for hours on end, we shall never know.

To go with this marvel of technology, the Wessex 5 was fitted with a truly remarkable UHF radio, the PTR 170. This was a lightweight set designed for the Whirlwind with the fantastic total of twelve crystallised channels and nothing else. The Whirlwind was lucky, as the set was not ready in time, but instead of ditching it, some communicator who clearly had a vested interest in the thing (probably future employment with the manufacturer, though anyone who would support the PTR 170 would make a doubtful employee!) kept the project alive and then bolted it into the Wessex 5, presumably thinking that's where it would do least harm. Even though twelve channels may have been adequate in the '60s and '70s, they were understandably always the wrong twelve channels.

Now you may think that 'junglies' have always enjoyed spending their lives flying as low as possible, but this is not so. We would have loved to join the 'pingers' flogging around in the clouds, idly glancing at instruments that patently lacked the correct attitudes, but we couldn't talk to anyone. The only answer was to keep as low as possible and talk to no one. After all, if you are lower than a delivery van, which does not have to get permission to enter the Heathrow Control Zone, why should you bother?

I had better clear up the low flying business, as the Wessex 5 spent most of its life there. To fly as low as possible is clearly still a prudent course of action, never mind the lack of radios that forced us down in the past. If anything drastic should go wrong, you are much closer to that which is going to break your fall. Just ask anyone who has fallen off a barn roof (as indeed I have) and he will tell you that 'height hurts'. Teaching students to fly the Wessex 5 was another interesting pastime, as anyone who has followed the saga of modifications to the fuel computers and the plethora of Pilot's Notes to go with them will testify. Luckily, once again the fantastic single-engine performance made up for any lack of speed in dealing with these things, while giving the instructor time to look up the correct actions as the student struggled with the wrong ones!

The total lack of drama when on one engine was well demonstrated by an experienced Pongo on an exchange posting. On his final handling check at the end of his conversion course he did autorotations, approaches, landings and take-offs, all without noticing that the port engine had not been advanced from 'ground idle', where it was no good to man or beast. On his re-scrub he did little better, so was returned to the Army where his single-engined flying skills were more appropriate for their single-engined aircraft.

The airframe did not always escape unscathed from these training exercises. Witness the two instructors who were practicing EOLs (Engine Off Landings) by pulling the Speed Select levers (throttles) back on each other in increasingly difficult places. One pulled them at 100 feet on climb out; the other chap realised things were beyond salvage and invited the perpetrator to sort things out! He was unable to intervene and failed to do anything positive, so the rotor RPM decayed drastically and they crashed straight ahead. The crew then had to climb out through the back of the cabin, as there was a main wheel gently rotating outside one pilot's window and the ground filling the other!

The Wessex 5 has certainly seen life all round the world, and its starring role in operations and disasters like the 1977 Fastnet Race during its history are well known. Its greatest asset was that it was fun to fly. You may not have been able to see much out of it; you may, even now, have a bad back from its appalling seats; you may well never have seen your crewman's face while in flight, but it was fun. You could chuck it about all you liked and just as long as you were smooth with your green-gloved mitts, it would do almost anything. Only retreating blade stall, tail rotor stall or your seat collapsing as the adjustor sprang out because of the vibration would let you know that its limits were being approached!

Will the Sea King 4, with its readily cracked airframe ever engender the same affection? With more radios than Currys, a 'defensive' suite that tells you you're being shot at, plus the bootnecks in the back able to see if you have got the right map, I doubt it. What about thirty degrees angle of bank the maximum, and vibration that would shake the spots off a raddled tart? Pah! Fancy not being able to land with over forty degrees nose up for fear of breaking something! The Commando assault at Air Days will never be the same again! Imagine, unlike the Wessex 5, not being able to fire rockets at your unarmed enemies. (Naturally we would never dare use them against someone who could fight back!)

No, we won't see the likes of her again, and more's the pity, but the venerable, lovable Wessex 5 was certainly amazing FUN while it lasted …

26 Putting the Record Straight

David Gibbings

The forward speed of the helicopter has never been the most important aspect. Igor Sikorsky famously said, 'Man wants to fly like a bird not a Bat out of Hell!'

In 1986, Westland was in trouble and its future in doubt. The company was embroiled in the 'Westland Affair' with a shortage of orders.

Strangely enough, its technical assets were high, and prominent amongst these were the new high-technology rotor blades, which were known by the strange acronym 'BERP' – British Experimental Rotor Profile.

It was well known that the blades would enhance the performance, and the designers believed that a significant improvement in forward speed could be demonstrated using a standard Lynx airframe, working within the rules laid down by the FAI (Fédération Aéronautique Internationale), to justify an attempt upon the absolute world speed record.

The Making of a Record Breaker (David Gibbings)

In the calm hazy evening of 11 August 1986, a Lynx helicopter flew over a measured 15 kilometre course, across the Somerset levels achieving an average speed of 400.87 kilometres per hour (249.10mph). In doing so it became the world's fastest helicopter. Although the machine which achieved the record had undergone a short modification programme to make it capable of such speeds, this basic airframe and rotor transmission were unchanged from that of the Lynx helicopter in service worldwide.

The story of the Lynx dates back to the early 1960s. The British aerospace industry had undergone a difficult period of contraction and rationalisation, during which many famous names had disappeared, leaving only two major aeroplane companies and a single helicopter manufacturer.

The Westland Aircraft Company had absorbed the helicopter interests of the Bristol Aircraft Co., the Fairey Aviation Company and Saunders-Roe Ltd, all of which became Westland Helicopters Ltd.

The British armed forces were at the time just beginning to appreciate the potential of the helicopter. The Royal Navy was taking delivery of the first Wasp, the Wessex anti-submarine helicopters were in service, the Commando Wessex Squadrons were embarked and the Whirlwind was well matured as a general workhorse. The Royal Air Force was equipping its support squadrons with Wessex which were supplemented by ageing Belvederes, while the backbone of its SAR capability was the Whirlwind. The Army was about to retire its Skeeters and take the Scout into service, and the Sioux was accepted to form the unit light helicopter and to be used as a basic trainer.

The British Government was looking to Europe as a way ahead for the future. It was against this turbulent backcloth that NGAST 6665 was issued, calling for a medium-sized helicopter suitable for all three services, for use in training, army utility and ship-borne roles with an all-up weight of 8000lb.

The Westland response to this requirement was project WG 13. The project underwent many revisions in size and shape before it was finalised for a Project Definition Study, by which time Britain's entry into Europe was committed. The move towards Europe led to an Anglo-French collaborative helicopter package, the basis for which was that the British services would accept Puma and Gazelle for support, training and light helicopter roles while the British WG 13 would be developed for the British and French services.

The ITP (Intention to Proceed) was announced in July 1967. The WG 13 programme was a massive undertaking. It involved twelve development prototype aircraft, this after an armed attack variant had been cancelled for the French Army. The new aircraft was to enter service as a utility helicopter for the British Army and as a ship-borne helicopter for both the Royal Navy and the Marine Nationale. The name Lynx was adopted in 1970 following a policy of using wild animal names for collaborative projects: Gazelle, Puma, Jaguar. The first flight of the Lynx prototype (XW835) took place on 21 March 1971, flown by the Chief Test Pilot, Ron Gellatly, with Roy Moxam as co-pilot. The Flight Test Engineer on this occasion was David Gibbings. The maiden flight ended a period of twenty-three years during which no new helicopter of all British design had flown.

The development programme continued throughout the five years that followed. The Royal Navy took delivery of its first Lynx in 1976 and the first Utility entered service with the Army Air Corps in 1977.

The twelve Lynx prototypes accumulated over 2,000 flying hours. In 1972 the Utility Lynx prototype (XX153) claimed two world speed records in its class: Class E.l.c, 3,000–4,500kg:

321.74 kilometres per hour (199.91mph) over 15km.

318.504 kilometres per hour (197.91mph) over 100km closed circuit.

The pilot was Roy Moxam assisted by Mike Ball as Flight Test Engineer.

In 1975 the Westland design team was awarded the McRobert Award by the Council of Engineering Institutions for innovative design with the Lynx rotor and transmission.

One of the most important features of the Lynx is its hingeless (semi-rigid) rotor head. The hub and blade arms are made of titanium, which allows blade movement in flap and lag to be absorbed by bending, dispensing with the customary hinges. The basic features of this rotor head remained unchanged on G-LYNX for its record flight.

For nearly four decades the Lynx has served with distinction. It is in service with nine navies and has seen active with the Royal Navy during the Falklands War, Iraq and worldwide anti-piracy operations, and with the UK land forces. Over 400 Lynx have been built and the Lynx design philosophy will continue with the AW159 Wildcat, which has a totally new composite airframe and an advanced central mission system.

The Rotor Technology (Geoffrey Byham)

To achieve the World Helicopter Speed Record in 1986 Westland needed to exceed 201kts over a 15km course. The company set itself the target of moving the speed record beyond the 400km barrier (216kts plus). At these speeds, at a practical achievable weight (around 8,000Ib) the normal Lynx rotor system would be flying well outside its stall envelope. In these conditions, large areas of separated flow exist on the rotor blades, creating unacceptable loads, drag and blade torsion, and therefore grossly degraded handling qualities.

The technology of the BERP blade has been developed to improve the useable flight envelope of the rotor by extending the conditions that can be achieved before stall or compressibility problems are encountered. This has been done in a number of ways: better aerofoils have been employed over the outer 30 per cent of the rotor blade to allow high angles of attack before local separation occurs. These sections are designed with geometries that accentuate the benefits of dynamic stall to recognise the special environment of the rotor blade.

RAE Farnborough and WHL worked together to define and create the right aerofoils for this task. The new outboard profiles were achieved by accepting the presence of a section pitching moment which, if left uncorrected, would create low-frequency torsional oscillations on the blade, affecting the aircraft handling and control.

A complementary aerofoil was therefore developed for inboard blade stations where both the incidence and local Mach number are not so critical. These relaxations allowed a reflex camber line to be used creating a cancelling pitching moment.

At the blade root, the unwanted oscillatory aerodynamic pitching moments were therefore brought to zero. As well as stall on the low speed parts of the rotor disc, the BERP blade geometry includes features to diminish the effects of high Mach number flows on the advancing blade tip.

The most visible feature is the tip planform which combines an element of sweep, which grows as local Mach number rises, with a forward area extension to reposition the mass and aerodynamic axes of the tip onto the pitch axis of the blade. The highly swept outermost edge is included to allow the tip to behave benignly at the very high angles of attack elsewhere on the rotor.

In fact the very stable flow created by this planform at high incidence allows great freedom in the choice of cross-sectional shape and therefore further compressibility benefits are obtained by combining it with a very thin aerofoil.

All of these aerodynamic steps allowed a very large improvement to the Lynx rotor envelope without changing the blade weight, area or tipspeed. The previous limitations of stall were extended by some 50kts for the speed record aircraft and this, together with the other modifications applied to G-LYNX, made the record possible.

Shaping up for the Record (John Perry)

The flight test programme which demonstrated the BERP Blade confirmed what all concerned with the project had always believed. The potential was such that an attempt on the Helicopter Absolute World Speed Record was a serious proposition.

The proposal was placed before the Westland Board. The Chairman, Sir John Cuckney, and the Chief Executive, Hugh Stewart, agreed that the attempt should proceed, as did the whole Board which included Don Berrington, who had been concerned with the blade development as Chief Designer and later as Technical Director during the design stage.

The whole undertaking became the responsibility of the Engineering Group under the Engineering Director, Richard Case, and the Chief Designer, Alan Vincent. The record attempt project was led by the Chief Engineer, Geoff Byham, supported by the Chief Aerodynamicist, John Perry. Success would be a dramatic demonstration of technical achievement. The Westland Company demonstrator Lynx helicopter, registered G-LYNX, was allocated to the task and a modest grant of private venture funding made available to incorporate the modifications necessary to support a drag and weight reduction programme and to refine the overall aerodynamic standard.

It was necessary to increase the installed power available from the Rolls-Royce Gem engines and to reduce the overall power consumption. The speeds envisaged represented new ground and a brief stress and handling assessment was required before embarking on the attempt. The whole exercise was approached as a serious technical exercise, leaving little to chance.

Lifting Capability, BERP Main Rotor Blades

One of the most important features of the BERP blade is its ability to support the helicopter at high speeds without stalling. The swept tip using thin aerofoil sections also helped to prevent power increases due to shock waves on the advancing blade tip under the high Mach number conditions anticipated during the record run.

The advanced manufacturing techniques, which Westland had developed working with composite materials, made it possible to make a blade in which the aerofoil cross-section was tailored to suit the regimen of flight under which the blade would have to function: a high lift, relatively low speed section in-board and a high speed (near sonic) section at the tip where the Mach number is high.

In the same way, it was possible to manufacture the blade spar to form the leading edge with considerable strength at the root tapering to a fine 9 per cent thickness/chord ratio at the tip.

Installed Power Increase

Installation of Gem 60 Engines

Flying fast requires high power, and the opportunity was taken to install the more powerful Rolls-Royce Gem 60 engines, which had been developed for the Westland 30. These engines could produce approximately 45 per cent more power than the original Gem engines with which the Lynx went into service.

Special Engine Ratings

In order to extract the highest power possible for the record flight, the engines were allowed to operate at emergency power levels not normally available to service aircraft. Rolls-Royce cleared the engines to operate at maximum contingency turbine inlet temperature levels for up to five minutes at a time and supported this clearance and other powerplant modifications with test bed endurance tests.

Water-Methanol Injection

To further boost engine power output, a water-methanol mixture was injected into the engine inlets through modified engine washing rings. The water-methanol lowers the gas stream temperature in the engine as it evaporates and allows higher powers to be produced for a given turbine inlet temperature limit. Engine compressor speed limits were also relaxed to make full use of this effect. The water-methanol mixture was contained in a modified long-range fuel tank installed within the cabin of the aircraft and provided enough mixture for multiple passes down the speed record course.

Up-rated Transmission

In order to transmit the extra engine power to the rotor, a main rotor gearbox, similar to that of the Westland 30, was introduced and allowed to run at Westland 30 emergency power levels. Even with this large increase in capability, the full power available from the engines could not be adequately transmitted to the rotor. In order that this power should not be wasted, a means was found to use it directly.

Anti-Torque and Yaw Control Capability

Offset Vertical Tailplanes and Low Set Stabiliser

The existing Lynx tail rotor was not capable of counteracting the increased torque supplied to the main rotor at the intended forward speed.

A low-set Westland 30 tailplane with offset vertical fins was therefore installed in order to carry a large portion of the tail rotor load at high speed. A small flap was also added to the central tail rotor pylon to help increase its side force.

Removal of Collective-Yaw Interlink

The carrying of the tail rotor load on fixed vertical surfaces reduced tail rotor pitch requirement with forward speed. In order to maintain comfortable pedal positions for the pilot, the usual yaw collective pitch interlink was removed. The aircraft was flown at zero sideslip in order to achieve the required trim forces on the fixed surfaces.

Reduction of Power Consumption

BERP Blades

Incorporation of BERP blades helped to contain the power consumption penalties felt by the rotor in high speed forward flight by reducing shock strength and consequent wave drag on the advancing blade, and by increasing the margin to retreating blade stall.

Drag Reduction

The major component of a helicopter's power consumption at high speed is from the parasite drag of the fuselage and rotor hub. Considerable reductions in drag relative to a service aircraft were obtained through detailed changes and fairings:

Rotor head fairings
Improved transmission cowling/fairing
Skid/undercarriage fairings
Door fairings
Removal of excrescences (steps, aerials, windscreen wipers etc.)
Sealing cracks and joints
Minimising momentum losses due to cooling flows

Comparison of Flight Results with Engineering Predictions

Many instrumented components were used in the preparation of G-LYNX for its World Speed Record attempt, and afforded the opportunity to collect test data under the most exacting flight conditions. It was found that rotor structural loads were very well predicted by theory, even at the highest speeds. It was demonstrated that the configuration changes, and in particular the dynamic design of the BERP rotor blades, made a dramatic improvement to the aircraft vibration characteristics at high speed. Aircraft power consumption was also very closely predicted, allowing the achieved record speed to be forecast to within 1km per hour.

The main rotor of the speed record aircraft, as well as many of its other novel features, will be incorporated into production aircraft and point the way to a new generation of high-speed and high-performance rotorcraft.

Facts for the Record

Speed Achieved: 400.87kph (249.1mph, 215.89knots)
Pilot: Trevor Egginton AFC, OBE
Flight Test Engineer: Derek Clews

27 The Westland Affair

David Gibbings

Of the many events that have taken place over the last century the 'Westland Affair' is one that will be long remembered and will continue to be the subject of debate for some time. David Gibbings was at Westland throughout, and gives his impression of what happened.

For Westland it was a defining moment; for those of us who were working hard for the company at the time, there was cause for concern and yet it was an exciting place to be. Most of us were working longer hours on interesting projects, with technology well in advance of anything we had seen.

In the early 1980s, the design phase of a new helicopter, the EH-101 was underway, and Westland composite blades were about to come to fruition, but these were all spending money, and our flagship product, the Westland 30, was not progressing well; computers were beginning to intrude on our working lives. As the Chinese proverb says, 'May you live in interesting times.'

It all began in 1984, a year of great literary significance. Throughout the whole of the 1970s Westland had experienced substantial growth and prosperity; the company's response to the Falklands War had demonstrated the value of our industry to the nation, and we hoped that it had been recognised.

Over 200 helicopters had gone south with the task force and all but a few had been built at Yeovil. Without them success would have been unlikely.

Work was in hand to replace the helicopters lost during the conflict. The design and development teams were in place to introduce a Sea King replacement, an exciting new helicopter, the EH-101, which was to be built as a collaborative deal, working with the Italian company Agusta. This in itself introduced a cultural change plus the introduction of a separate company, European Helicopter Industries, to 'manage the programme'.

In the late 1970s, Westland had embarked on a programme to introduce a civil helicopter based on the Lynx transmission; this in itself was unusual. During its time as a fixed-wing manufacturer Westland had never produced a civil aircraft in any quantity and although the various Sikorsky/Westland derivatives had sold on the civil market, these had evolved from military variants, with Sikorsky holding the overall design authority.

The configuration of the new aircraft was excellent, with a capacious cabin which offered comfortable seating. There were a few shortcomings; primarily the lynx transmission had been designed for military use. The semi-rigid rotor was an expensive item to produce and would have to be fully certified for civilian use, which in itself could prove to be a costly process. The military criteria for vibration levels were not necessarily satisfactory for a civil aircraft.

By 1984 there were already a number of Westland 30s in service; British Airways were operating the aircraft, investigating its potential on transport routes and within the oil industry; and there was some overseas interest, particularly in the USA, the most promising of these being 'Airspur' which was set up to operate a service to and from Los Angeles Airport (LAX), operating from nearby locations to service long-haul flights. In other areas the expected take-up of overseas orders was slow, and there were several development issues to be resolved – vibration levels were high and proving to be difficult to reduce to an acceptable level, and a US requirement for helicopters to taxi with the fixed-wing aircraft when positioning on the airfield presented a problem. The unique ability of the helicopter to position itself by flight, known as 'hover taxying', also disturbed debris with the rotor downwash and the risk of FOD (Foreign Object Damage) to other aircraft. The proposed solution involved substantial mileage taxying on the ground, which was a totally unexpected requirement; landing gear maintenance arising from this activity could be frequent and expensive, and would require additional design work.

Late in 1983 Airspur had a major accident, losing the aircraft and injuring passengers.

Westland were also working hard to raise military interest in the Westland 30 but to no avail; the situation became further complicated when the post-Falkland's order for replacements was substantially smaller than expected.

The EH-101 was unlikely to be in production, to produce a worthwhile income, before 1990; the prospect was for a low income from manufacturing against a high expenditure.

The financial institutions made it clear that although Westland was technically strong, it would need a strong financial partner to see it through the lean years ahead. As time progressed it became apparent that the national economy was about to take the downturn and the need for Westland to find a good business partner became even more urgent.

The British media was quick to sense that there was a problem and set about to 'help' the situation by references to 'the troubled West Country helicopter firm...'

This led to an unwelcome bid by entrepreneur Alan Bristow, who dominated the Oil Industry Flight Operations, and was confident that he could succeed with Westland.

The Westland board were in the process of negotiating with Sikorsky who already held a major stake in Westland; the company had always felt comfortable working with Sikorsky, but there was a powerful group at Westminster who felt that the European option should be considered, in order to strengthen the impression that the UK was fully committed in its drive to become an effective part of the European Union. The Secretary of State for Defence, Michael Heseltine, was a strong advocate of this.

So it was that the scene was set for a major crisis. Westland was finding it difficult to market their current product range; their expenditure was high in all areas of development, in that the Westland 30 venture was breaking new ground by attempting entry to the civil market, the programme was entering the complex and expensive certification phase, and it would be some time before any return from the investment could be expected.

The Indian Navy, with its large order for Sea Kings, was proving to be a difficult and demanding customer, ready to take full advantage of the situation. The Mk 42B they had ordered was a whole order of complexity beyond anything they had seen, and the whole ethos within the service was proving slow to adapt. The fact that the Indian Navy retained a wall of truculent mistrust of its contractors also gave cause for concern.

The Sea King replacement was to be the EH-101; a joint venture working with the Italian company Agusta, it was clear that there would be no substantial return for some time to come.

Westland were achieving groundbreaking success in their approach to composite blade design but again it would be some time before the new product could be on the market, and in the meantime the work involved would call for high expenditure.

The political situation was no less complicated. The government was committed to membership of the European Union, which appeared to be extending its powers beyond that expected when the UK first joined. Opinion at Westminster was divided. Margaret Thatcher would have her work cut out simply to maintain party unity without having to consider the needs of a 'Small Country Town'.

By the end of 1984 the situation at Westland was looking serious, and the board of Westland were searching for a backer to support them through the lean years.

In the Middle East, Saudi Arabia was in the process of upgrading their air force. BAE Systems was well advanced on the biggest arms contract they had ever experienced, involving Tornado and Eurofighter jets in formidable quantities. There was now talk of extending the programme to include helicopters. The preferred helicopter was the Sikorsky Blackhawk, but US manufacturers were barred by Congress from taking part in arms deals in the Middle East. Sikorsky was one of Westland's largest shareholders, and negotiations opened up for Westland to build Blackhawks.

Needless to say, all the unwelcome media activity resulted in a loss of confidence in the Westland management, which resulted in a major shake-up and several resignations.

At government level, sensing the serious implications, Margaret Thatcher proposed that Westland should agree that Sir John Cuckney be accepted as chairman.

But all was not well at Cabinet level; Michael Heseltine was convinced that Westland was heading for a full American takeover, and clearly felt that this would not be looked upon with any favour by our European partners. Westland, on the other hand, were well satisfied as all their previous ventures with Sikorsky had always gone smoothly and proved to be profitable. They had no such confidence that it would be possible to work effectively with Aerospatiale, the French company that had been their partner on the Lynx/Gazelle/Puma programme.

'The Westland Affair' became a national issue that dominated the news throughout 1985. At cabinet level, opinions were divided; Michael Heseltine and his supporters favoured an arrangement whereby BAE Systems and Westland would enter an agreement to integrate their activities with Aerospatiale and Agusta, presenting a strong European industry.

The prime minister and her trade and industry secretary, Leon Brittan, preferred to allow Westland to find its own solution, which entailed closer integration with Sikorsky.

Things came to a head in January 1986, when Heseltine resigned his position as Secretary of State for Defence.

The surprise resignation embarrassed the prime minister and divided opinions throughout her government. In the debate that followed, Leon Brittan resigned because he felt that he no longer had the full confidence of his colleagues.

The activity at government level was such that the very foundations of the government were shaken.

At the cabinet meeting on 9 January 1986, Michael Heseltine resigned with the statement 'I can no longer be a member of this Cabinet', and then stormed out of No.10, announcing his action to the waiting press.

Leon Brittan resigned following the debate on 23 January, stating: 'It has become clear to me that I no longer command the full confidence of my colleagues.'

Sensing that all was not well within the government ranks, the opposition called for a debate on 27 January during which the government and Margaret Thatcher took a mauling.

Westland, in the meantime, had undergone a significant rearrangement at board level under Sir John Cuckney's leadership and negotiated an agreement with Sikorsky whereby the American company would acquire a 29.9 per cent shareholding and an agreement to build the Blackhawk for the Middle East market; they would also support Westland with a substantial amount of subcontract work.

In the months that followed, Westland underwent a major reorganisation at all levels, including not only management and staff, but the whole organisational infrastructure accompanied by a large redundancy programme; some 800 loyal employees lost their jobs, with no indication that they had worked or performed badly.

This in itself was significant. Throughout the first half of the 1980s there had been clear signs of a world trade recession. It finally came in 1988, by which time Westland had reorganised to become 'lean, mean and ready'.

If the Westland crisis had not occurred when it did, the probability is that Westland may well have been one of the casualties. As it was, the company entered the 1990s with a good product base in the form of EH-101 Merlin, Apache, Lynx, blade technology and avionics capability.

Personal Comment

I worked at Westland throughout this period. Strangely enough, it was a good place to be; the personal relationships within the organisation were excellent, stirred on by a sort of 'Dunkirk spirit' and confidence that the company's product was sound. Morale was high.

The name Westland was everywhere, I even got a sympathetic upgrade to first class on one of my trips to India at the time. The restructuring process was painful, as many of our close friends and colleagues lost their jobs. It is the nature of such things that many of the people affected were close to retirement, having contributed a great deal towards success during their working life, and no matter how lucrative the compensation proves to be, there is a feeling of rejection. It is no way to finish a life's work.

There were a few tears that day and most of us would not wish to see it repeated.

Thirty years later, Westland is the British arm of an Italian company; perhaps the interesting times are still with us.

28 Working with the Italians/English

Peter Dunford and Fiorenzo Mussi

It seems hard to believe that for one third of the century that is the subject of this celebration, Westland has been working closely with Italian company Agusta and since the turn of the century the two companies have joined as one under the name AgustaWestland.

The result is that there has been a mingling of cultures between staff at all levels, and our 'Quiet Country Town' has changed even further.

The defining moment was when the two companies agreed to work together as equal partners to produce a Sea King replacement. Having already experienced collaborative working with the Anglo-French Collaborative Agreement, we all thought we knew what to expect.

Peter Dunford was involved at the beginning and spent the rest of his working life with the project; he and his friend Fiorenzo Mussi take up the story.

It all started in 1980 with an agreement between the British and Italian governments to procure a replacement helicopter for the aging Sea King and SN-3D helicopters in use with British and Italian navies.

This replacement helicopter, designated the EH-101, was to be designed, developed and productionised jointly between the two nations' helicopter companies, Westland Helicopter of the UK and Agusta Spa of Italy.

This helicopter was required to incorporate state-of-the-art technology, have the built-in capacity to allow mid-life updates and was to be a joint project to be equally shared in cost, technology and manufacturing between the two nations.

The process was initially started with the two companies independently identifying which parts of the work share they were best equipped to undertake.

Work sharing agreements were eventually thrashed out following numerous very difficult, frustrating and sometimes impossible meetings; this was to be the beginning of a complex and often frustrating, but eventually a very rewarding relationship between the two companies.

This is the story as experienced by two senior engineers from Agusta Spa and Westland Helicopters. Fiorenzo Mussi an experienced rotor designer, who through this period rose to become the Italian design leader, and Peter Dunford, an experienced Flight Test Engineer, Chief Development Engineer and ultimately Project Executive at EHI.

Fiorenzo defines this period in his career as the 'Against Period' or the period of exploration and understanding.

The Work Share

It is probably worthwhile at this juncture to briefly explain the work share arrangement between the two companies working on the EH-101.

The design, development and manufacture of the prototype aircraft was split evenly between the two companies, with neither being the lead.

To overcome this lack of leadership a separate organisation was formed to provide guidance, focus and to resolve any conflicts that existed. This company also formed the management interface between the companies and the Italian and British governments.

The organisation was called European Helicopter Industries (EHI) and was made up of representatives of both Agusta and Westland and was based in London.

The Beginning of a Relationship

An Italian Perspective or 'The Against Period' (Fiorenzo Mussi)

In the beginning, working with the English was a sufficiently traumatic experience and not what I was accustomed to with other foreign partners, Americans, French and German on short-term assignments of rotor or rotor-associated projects.

The new situation we the Italians faced immediately appeared more difficult as there were major differences in working practices, working methods, different organisation structures and lines of responsibility, different decision-making processes, different legal requirements, design standards etc.

Moreover, an equally difficult problem was one of communication; the English, as they are referred to by Italians which encompasses Scottish, Welsh and Irish, have a basic and significant advantage in the relationship, causing a feeling of inferiority and apprehension amongst the Italian community.

Whilst the project language was agreed to be English – for most of the Agusta employees, English had been acquired whilst working in collaboration with American companies – there was a significant shortfall in understanding and plenty of scope for misinterpretation. This was a two-way problem and caused numerous arguments and disagreements in the early days of working together.

This language difficulty, coupled with other cultural differences – driving on the left, food, currency, religion, even dress and warm beer – created in the Italians a feeling of discomfort, unease and a sense of inferiority.

Such a complex design could not be realised without a total and indiscriminate reciprocal trust and, as both teams were highly intelligent and rational people, it was inevitable that eventually reason and common sense would prevail.

There was, however, at times and in certain situations an attitude of superiority by the English community which did nothing to promote integration.

An English Perspective (Peter Dunford)

My first involvement with another European Aerospace Company was in the late 1960s with Sud Aviation, later to become Aerospatiale. Westland at that time was involved in the development and production of the Gazelle and Puma helicopters for the British armed forces.

Sud Aviation owned the design of these vehicles and Westland involvement was only one aspect of adaptation to meet the British military's specific requirements, consequently the relationship was one of master and follower.

This experience initially coloured my view towards co-operation with European companies, in that UK processes and practices were deemed as inadequate with all decisions being made in France, the majority of meetings were in France and the English team was most definitely subservient to the French. Fortunately my experience working with Agusta was soon to change these views.

My first involvement with Agusta was with the design and manufacture of the flight trials instrumentation package. The first hurdle to overcome was not only the language but also the interpretation of the language, the project language being English. It became very evident at these initial meetings that we were separated by the interpretation of a common language.

The Italians complained that the English spoke too quickly such that they couldn't keep up with the discussion and often misunderstood, whilst the biggest complaint by the English was that the Italians held discussions between themselves in Italian, leaving the English wondering what the debates were all about. This was not conducive of creating an atmosphere of trust and collaboration; however, these early teething troubles were soon behind us.

Agusta's personnel experience of working in the English language was with American companies, namely Boeing, Sikorsky and Bell, as previously stated by Fiorenzo.

Misunderstanding became commonplace, which at times created tensions, mistrust and numerous heated and fractious debates. However with time these barriers were overcome, but at the expense of losing valuable project time.

The next hurdle which proved to be much more difficult to resolve was the different approaches to gathering flight data and the analysis of this data. Each company had its own proven systems, which were in use on all their other platforms. These two systems were incompatible and raw data could not be transferred between them as the format for the collection of the data was different.

Neither company was prepared to analyse data on the other's behalf so a stalemate situation soon arose. After many months of deliberation and posing by both sides, a solution was found; the solution was neither elegant nor inexpensive, but nevertheless it allowed the programme to continue.

In the early days of the programme, situations like this were commonplace as there was apparent distrust by both parties and a lack of will to compromise, the consequence being prolonged timescales to get decisions, leading to lengthy programme delays and inherent cost escalation.

In keeping with the work share agreement, the flight trials of the basic vehicle was split equally between the two companies, whilst the customisation for the respective national military variants was undertaken separately by each company.

It became apparent during the early days of the flight development programme that the solutions to the technical problems encountered were being treated differently by the two companies; this initially led to lack of commonality between the Italian and British vehicle platforms.

Each engineering team believed that it had the most elegant and cost-effective solution to the problems encountered.

The situation could not be allowed to continue and a solution had to be found; it was at this juncture that it was agreed by all parties, including the respective governments, to form an organisation called 'Single Site'.

It was this action that merged the two engineering organisations into a dedicated focused activity to resolve the technical issues.

This was the start of my total immersion into Italian life and working practices, and proved to be an invaluable experience both for me and the programme, and for my family who accompanied me to live for two years in northern Italy.

The Together Period or Full Collaboration

After enduring the situation as defined in the 'Against Period' section – it was as a miracle for those who believe in miracles or as a consequence of a more realistic and rational evaluation – we found ourselves in a new phase of relationship, which is defined as the 'Together Period'. How long did the previous period last? Well this is subject to speculation: for some a few days, for others weeks or months and others maybe it still exists today.

Actually, the duration is determined by the capability of each of us to discover a fundamental aspect, based upon our ability to interpret the situation and circumstances with our partner and to adapt to the cultural differences.

An example of this … the most evident one was driving as Italians drive on the right and English drive on the left; this was not a significant problem for the English as most of us who holiday abroad are faced with driving on the other side of the road and therefore it is not as alien.

However, for the Italians it was often their first experience and therefore somewhat daunting; in addition, speed restriction enforcement is much more rigorous in the UK, but lane discipline is far worse. Italians always give way on multi-lane carriageways to faster-moving traffic, which is definitely not the case in England.

Many other lifestyle differences existed, simple things like restaurants; twenty years ago pizzerias in Yeovil were non-existent, and Indian food was initially far too spicy for the Mediterranean taste. English beer is warm whereas Italian beer is always served cold.

For those of us who spent time living in northern Italy with our families, the cultural differences were immense and often created domestic unrest.

Paying household bills such as refuse collection had to be done in conjunction with paying for a dog licence at the local council offices and could take hours filling out copious forms in triplicate.

Paying utility bills was just as tedious and could take the best part of a day.

We English pride ourselves on being well organised, with well-documented processes and procedures, which are in general adhered to.

Not so in Italy; there appears never to be a detailed plan or a procedure, just an end goal, which will be reached eventually, a bit like driving in Italy.

These are just a few examples of the subtle differences that existed between the two countries at that time, differences that appear on the face of it insignificant, but hugely important to maintain a motivated work force.

At this point, the consideration that appears more appropriate is no longer working with Italians, but living with the Italians.

Once we all realised and accepted the cultural and lifestyle differences and consequently modified our approach to one another, we were no more driven by the work to be done together; the real new driving concept became living with one another, and work became an important by-product of this new relationship.

There were groups of Italians resident in Yeovil and groups of English resident in Cascina Costa on long-term assignments; in addition, there was a significant number of both nationalities travelling back and forth to meetings and conferences.

The integration process described became possible because, under the surface, our cultures are fundamentally similar; the differences identified at the beginning of the partnership, that were considered insuperable, became so unfounded and simply became a joke.

The respect and understanding between the partnership started to crystallise to the point when Single Site was created and true companionship was realised.

Single Site and the Marriage of Agusta and Westland Engineers

Single Site working consisted of a group of Westland and Italian engineers co-located in Cascina Costa together with the first two prototype aircraft and associated test rigs, their task being to develop the basic vehicle to a standard fit for production within a two-year timescale.

The Agusta factory and airfield at Cascina Costa was chosen for this activity, primarily as the transmission was immature and required frequent maintenance, and as it was designed and built in Cascina Costa it made economic sense for the trials aircraft to be located close to the facility. The weather is also much better in northern Italy, being on the leeward side of the Alpine mountain range, and this would lead to higher flying rates and hence faster progress.

This co-location at first proved to be very difficult, not only from the work perspective but also for family life.

There were two groups from Westland, those with families who had chosen to live and work in Italy for the whole period of the assignment and those who preferred to work on a three-month rotation, leaving their families back in England.

The hurdles to be overcome were the language barrier, followed by the cultural differences both in and outside of the workplace, differences in engineering philosophy and procedures, schooling integration into the Italian community and, not least of all, driving.

The wives and children found integration into the Italian way of life, in shopping, schooling, driving etc., frustrating and difficult; this had an adverse impact on the workforce and added to the everyday problems getting the work done.

Even though the two teams were co-located and were operating as one team, as the UK prototype was a British asset it had to be operated in accordance with British Ministry of Defence rules. This was not the case for the Italian assets, and proved to be a significant issue, especially for Agusta, as they struggled to understand the concept of the UK government's insistence on the UK assets being operated under UK military rules.

The first six months were very difficult and frustrating, with little progress being made; there was distrust on both sides often fuelled by ignorance and misunderstanding.

Those with families were often preoccupied in solving schooling, housing and other problems associated with integration into an Italian community and were therefore not wholly concentrating on their reason for being in Italy. This was fully understandable and was a period we had to get through for this unique experiment to work effectively.

In order to get through this initial period, we introduced informal gatherings outside of the workplace with our Italian counterparts; visits from the British Consul in Milan plus visits from managers from Yeovil were also instigated.

In addition, most of the wives joined an expatriates club called 'Bienvenuto', which organised coffee mornings, mountain walks, advice on integration and general help on the integration issue, and friendship.

Lessons on the Italian language and culture were also introduced in order to ease the integration process.

The engineering processes utilised by Westland were far more stringent and rigid when compared to that in use by Agusta; most of these processes employed by Westland were dictated to by the UK Ministry of Defence rules for military projects.

As the Agusta element of the team were not under the same restraints they were able to make engineering changes and progress faster, this in turn caused a degree of frustration within the British contingent as they saw their hands tied and felt not in a position to fully contribute initially. With time came greater understanding, which created trust and co-operation between the two groups.

The work ethic between Agusta and Westland at that time was also very different and it took a while for both groups to come to terms with the differences.

The Westland approach was to make progress as quickly as possible, as goals and deadlines had to be achieved. Agusta were much more laid back and less inclined to see major milestones as the God to be obeyed.

Westland were very much driven by planning, plans, achievements of objectives and intermediate milestones; Agusta, on the other hand, appeared to be mainly interested in the final objective and not so interested in the route to achieving this.

Detailed planning and programmes are a big part of the Westland and British culture, whereas Agusta take a much higher-level approach to the process and rely less on low-level detail. To my knowledge this has never been resolved between the two organisations and the differences still exist today, but in true collaboration both groups accept the differences.

Another aspect worth noting is the need to demonstrate to the Italians integrity and trust; once you gained their confidence and respect you became accepted by them and ultimately became a friend for life.

One characteristic of the Italians in meetings was to have a side meeting in Italian, leaving the Westland members wondering what was going on; however, as our ability to understand Italian improved, this characteristic became less of an annoyance.

Another common characteristic of the Italians, which was completely alien to the English community and took a while to understand and indeed appreciate, is that Italians are often a very excitable and passionate people who will have extremely heated arguments with one another, with much gesticulation and sometimes the use of obscenities. Once the disagreement is over, it's all forgotten, there is no bad blood between them, and they revert back to the way the situation was before the argument – very different to the reserved British reaction in similar situations.

The English people have a propensity to drink large quantities of alcohol, often to achieve a highly drunken state. This approach to alcohol is alien to Italians by and large and as such we as a nation have a bad reputation for being drunken, unruly, disorderly and aggressive, epitomised by the behaviour of football hooligans – this being particularly true in the 1980s.

Unfortunately, during the early stages of Single Site some members of the Westland team demonstrated this behavioural characteristic, which did nothing to assist in the integration process, either in the workplace or the community. This continues to be an unfortunate characteristic of the British when overseas.

There was one occasion when I had to rescue a number of the team from the clutches of the police after a drunken night out which resulted in disorderly behaviour; luckily this was a one-off occurrence and was never repeated.

Most Italians enjoy wine and cold beer purely for the enjoyment, not to get drunk.

I am in no doubt that the Single Site experience cemented the relationship between Westland and Agusta engineers into one of mutual respect, both on a professional and personal footing; most of the English members of that team have many Italian friends and quite a few of them now work permanently in Italy.

Much of the success of the EH-101 can be attributed to the engineering solutions derived by the engineers of the Single Site team.

An Italian colleague of mine expressed to me in later years that the Single Site activity was the high point of his engineering career, a true accolade indeed for collaboration and trust across national boundaries.

Living in Italy

Living in Italy in the late 1980s without today's modern communications, mobile phones, Internet, Sky TV etc. was not easy, especially for the wives and families.

Integration into the local community, shopping, schooling, paying bills, driving, dentist etc. and all the other day-to-day activities we do and take for granted become a challenge when and if you don't speak the language.

Most families managed the transition into an Italian lifestyle. There was, however, the odd exception, who could not adjust and had to return to the UK.

Having made the transition, returning to the UK was a cultural shock in reverse.

The families who accompanied us enjoyed a very different lifestyle, which was varied, culturally stimulating and exciting; most of the children and wives returned home speaking some if not fluent Italian, and there is little doubt that the education system offered to the children was far superior to that in the UK at that time.

The climate, lifestyle, food, culture, history and general standard of living for engineers was higher in Italy and this all helped with the integration into the community, and the spin-off from contented families reflected in the performance in the workplace. There was a multitude of recreational facilities available, most of which did not exist in the proximity of Yeovil; skiing in the winter was about an hour away, as was mountain walking in the summer. The Italian lakes were within a thirty-minute drive, as was the fashion and shopping capital Milan; the Mediterranean coast was only a four-hour drive, as was the Adriatic coast and Venice.

The climate, we must not forget the climate, had lovely cold crisp sunny winter days and hot and balmy summer days; the windy weather associated with England was very rare in the area where we lived, which as I stated earlier was on the leeward side of the Alpine mountain range.

Initially, driving on the wrong side of the road was a challenge, as were some of the rules of the road; the giving way rule at roundabouts was troublesome at first, as was the approach to driving in fog and traffic lights.

Driving bumper to bumper at high speed in fog was also the norm, and when I queried that surely this is dangerous, the reply was, the closer the gap, the less the impact!

My first experience of driving in Rome resulted in me asking a question of the receptionist at the hotel I was staying as to why at some road junctions drivers choose to ignore the red lights.

The answer was simple; there are so many traffic lights in Rome it is impossible to stop at all of them, so therefore you continue with a degree of caution. Why didn't I think of that?

Final Words

Working with Italians in the UK and Italy was a privilege and a life-changing experience for me, my family and for all who participated from both the English and Italian communities. In addition to the obvious benefits achieved to the programme, by the engineering solutions found and the progress made, the individuals involved enjoyed a very rich cultural and gastronomic experience into the Italian way of life, the memories of which will last a lifetime.

The friendships made some twenty-five years ago still endure to this day, which speaks volumes for the benefits of cross-cultural programmes; 'where there is a will there is always a way'.

It was inevitable as a result of market forces that eventually the two companies would merge and I am convinced that the experience and knowledge gained through the Single Site exercise made that process easier and simpler. Many of the problems and pitfalls encountered by the integration of two differing cultures had been experienced and overcome, lesson learned and documented.

Finally, when two great companies come together and share skills, experience, understanding, mutual respect and intellect, there is no limit to what can be achieved.

In Memorium

Some time after the Single Site team returned from Italy, the Italian prototype crashed killing all four crew members. The sense of loss and mutual grief that this event caused was devastating; I and the Single Site team were hit very hard, but many of the Yeovil team were also marked by the tragedy.

In conclusion, Fiorenzo and I would like to dedicate this dialogue to 'our' friends and colleagues:

Raffaele Longobardi
Gilberto Tintori
Massimo Colombo
Stefano Novelli

29 Airfield Noise!

David Gibbings

The design, development and manufacture of aircraft have taken place at the Yeovil site since 1915. During that time the management and structure of the company responsible has undergone several changes, but the fundamental business as an aircraft manufacturer has continued, uninterrupted, for a full century, with the distinction that trading has continued under the name Westland.

Established during the 1914–18 war, it was considered to be outside the town boundary, and was probably looked upon as a temporary wartime necessity. One hundred years later, it is surrounded by houses. A summary and a few final comments by David Gibbings.

At the turn of the century (1800–1900), Yeovil was the centre of the British Glove Industry; there was, however, a privately owned industrial company, Petter Oil Engines, established in 1899 that by the outbreak of the 1914–1918 war had developed into a major manufacturer of utility engines, with an output of 1,500 engines per year.

As the war progressed during 1914, it quickly became apparent that the industrial capacity to maintain the war effort would have to increase.

The board of Petters responded by offering to undertake armament work in any capacity within their capability.

The response to this offer came from the Admiralty, with a requirement for Short 184 seaplanes and a commitment for follow-up orders. The result was that Petters established the factory and airfield on the current site at what was then the outskirts of Yeovil.

Once established, the new aircraft works grew rapidly, and by the end of hostilities, had evolved into a properly founded aircraft company with full design and development capability. During the four years of war, the Westland works produced over 800 aircraft, including Sopwith 1½ Strutters, DH-9 and Vickers Vimys, but had also developed its own design capability.

The expected growth of civil aviation following the war failed to materialise, and the large British aircraft industry that had grown up as a result now found it difficult to survive. Westland was fortunate in that it had become the design authority for the DH-9A, an aircraft that had been retained by the RAF for its worldwide Commonwealth commitments; the subsequent adoption of their DH-9-based Wapiti assured the company's survival during the difficult years between the two world wars.

The design team at Westland was both innovative and prolific in output, producing a range of interesting developments:

The Widgeon monoplane light aircraft in 1925.
The Wizard monoplane fighter in 1926.
The Interceptor and C.O.W. gun monoplane fighters in 1929.
The first flight over the summit of Mount Everest in 1933.
The Hill Pterodactyl series of tailless aircraft, 1928–34.

In the mid-1930s, the Westland design organisation became the responsibility of W.E.W. Petter. It was under his leadership that several famous Westland aircraft were designed, namely Lysander, the Whirlwind twin-engined fighter and Welkin, the high-altitude fighter.

After leaving Westland in 1953, Petter went on to design the Canberra bomber, the preliminary design for the Lightning fighter and subsequently the Folland Gnat.

Another famous name associated with Westland was that of Harald Penrose, who held the post of Chief Test Pilot from 1930 to 1953, spanning the biplane era to the jet age, to become one of the great airmen of our time.

The Welkin high-altitude fighter achieved some groundbreaking success in the field of cabin pressurisation, which resulted in the founding of 'Normalair' as a subsidiary of Westland, specialising in cabin conditioning.

At the outbreak of the Second World War, Westland was a centre for Spitfire production, which took on even more importance when the Supermarine works at Southampton was destroyed by bombing.

Westland and a few other hastily set up factories were the main source for Spitfires and repairs during the 'Battle of Britain'. As the war progressed, Westland became the prime source and design authority for the Seafire (Naval variant of the Spitfire). A total of 2,200 Spitfire/Seafires were produced at Yeovil during the war years.

In 1948, the Westland board made a policy decision to concentrate all future activities on the design, development and production of helicopters. In order to facilitate this, an agreement was made with the American company Sikorsky to build their S-51 helicopter under licence; during the ten years that followed, the agreement was extended to include S-55 and S-58, by which time Westland was established as a major helicopter company.

In 1960, the British government made it clear that aircraft companies would have to join together into larger units if they were to be considered acceptable to undertake defence contracts. There followed what was considered to be 'mayhem' within the industry. The twenty or so fixed-wing companies amalgamated into two large groups, leaving only a few isolated dissenting firms.

There were only four companies specialising in rotorcraft, Bristol, Fairey, Saunders-Roe and Westland, and of these Westland were by far commercially the strongest, having concentrated their activities on production and sales. The result was that Westland absorbed the other three, to become the UK's sole helicopter manufacturer.

The enlarged company took on responsibility for Belvedere, Sycamore, Rotodyne and Scout/Wasp helicopters, and also extended the Sikorsky licence to include the Sea King.

In the 1970s, Westland responded to a UK requirement for a range of military helicopters, which resulted in the Anglo-French Helicopter Deal, through which the UK accepted Puma and Gazelle, but which also included the British-designed Lynx.

The Lynx was intended for service with the Army and the Royal Navy, and included a number of innovative features such as:

A highly responsive semi-rigid rotor.
A low profile gearbox, incorporating 'conformal' gears.
An integrated deck landing system, which included a harpoon deck-securing device and the ability to apply negative collective pitch to hold on the deck prior to final restraint.

Coming from the experience gained with the Wasp, the Lynx can justifiably claim to have set the pattern for all small ships' deck operations.

As the Lynx has matured, several further features have been developed, including the British Experimental Rotor Programme (BERP) rotor blades. The composite construction techniques and advanced technology incorporated in these blades made it possible to achieve a Helicopter World Speed Record of 250mph/400.17kph.

In the late 1970s, work began to consider a replacement for the Sea King anti-submarine helicopter. The Italian government had a requirement for a similar aircraft. Early in 1980 negotiations were opened with the Italian company Agusta to undertake a Joint Venture to build a suitable helicopter, and European Helicopter Industries Ltd was formed to manage the programme for the design and development of the project, then known as EH-101.

Over the last two decades, the ties between Westland and Agusta have strengthened and culminated with the formation of AgustaWestland, as an equal partner joint venture and in 2005 AgustaWestland became part of Finmeccanica.

Yeovil continues to serve as the centre for the provision and support for helicopters for the British armed forces, and holds its place as exporter of rotorcraft and associated activities.

Westland continues to advance rotorcraft technology from this site as part of AgustaWestland. During its time as a fixed-wing aircraft company, it played no small part in the transition to the space age, and over 6,000 aircraft were built here.

In the sixty years that Westland has functioned as a helicopter company, this site and the engineers who work here can justifiably be recognised as the heart of rotorcraft development in the UK.

Of the 3,000+ helicopters built in Britain, some 2,500 were manufactured on this site.

A chart showing the way in which rotorcraft have developed in Britain, and the significant contribution that has taken place under the Westland name, with Yeovil at its centre, has been added as Figure 1. This also shows links that extend back in rotorcraft history to include Cierva and Hafner.

The airfield and works at Yeovil have been recognised by the Royal Aeronautical Society as a World Aviation Heritage Site.

This global recognition is the culmination of a century of aviation activity and should give rise to considerable civic pride that 'a quiet country town' can play such a significant part in the world-changing technology that has evolved in little more than a century.

Where there is an airfield, there is aircraft noise, and this is not always favourably received. Because of its close proximity to the town, houses have gradually surrounded the Yeovil airfield, and it is not surprising that the noise generated is a common complaint from residents, and it does not help to argue that the airfield has been there for the best part of a century.

Being a test airfield, most of the activity has taken place during the working week, and a house viewed during a weekend can appear to be all that can be hoped for when moving to 'a quiet country town'.

The arrival of helicopters has aggravated the situation; they tend to hang around, especially when they are on test, and even those of us who have been directly responsible for generating the noise in the course of our work sometimes find it disturbing.

Author's Comment

Westland has made its mark on Yeovil; few families have lived here for any time without some relative working there. It has always been involved in the front line of technology.

The emergence of Westland as an aircraft company has transformed Yeovil from a quiet country town to the focal point of rotorcraft development in the UK.

I for one am proud to have played a small part in it.

Perhaps when the sound of the occasional flight test breaks into the evening or weekend tranquillity, all assuming that it is not the Air Ambulance on its errand of mercy, maybe we should consider:

'Helicopter noise, is the sound of local prosperity!'

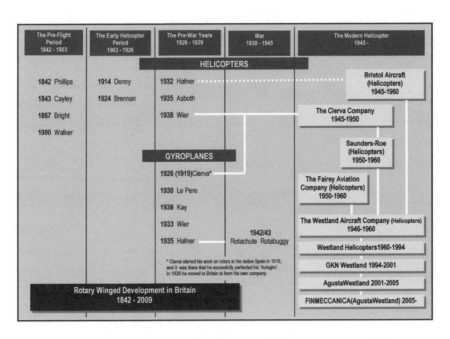

Figure 1: This chart was produced as part of the presentation for the European Rotorcraft Forum in Hamburg. It shows how the industry has developed in the UK.

Appendix 1: Aircraft List

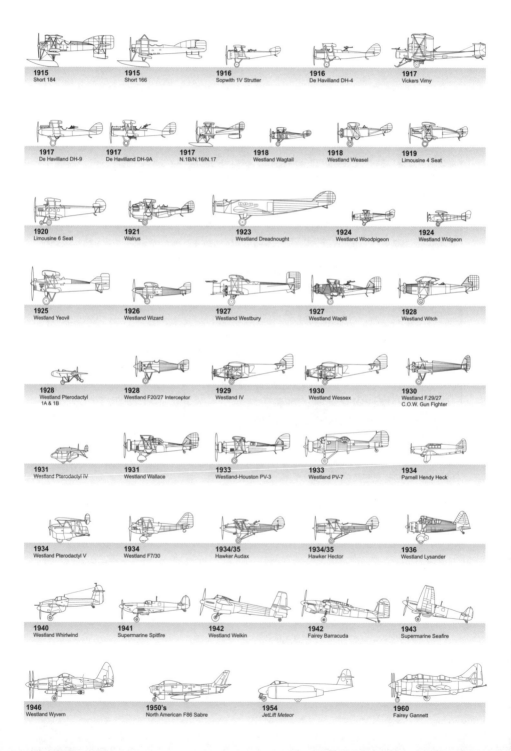

1915 Short 184

1915 Short 166

1916 Sopwith 1V Strutter

1916 De Havilland DH-4

1917 Vickers Vimy

1917 De Havilland DH-9

1917 De Havilland DH-9A

1917 N.1B/N.16/N.17

1918 Westland Wagtail

1918 Westland Weasel

1919 Limousine 4 Seat

1920 Limousine 6 Seat

1921 Walrus

1923 Westland Dreadnought

1924 Westland Woodpigeon

1924 Westland Widgeon

1925 Westland Yeovil

1926 Westland Wizard

1927 Westland Westbury

1927 Westland Wapiti

1928 Westland Witch

1928 Westland Pterodactyl 1A & 1B

1928 Westland F20/27 Interceptor

1929 Westland IV

1930 Westland Wessex

1930 Westland F.29/27 C.O.W. Gun Fighter

1931 Westland Pterodactyl IV

1931 Westland Wallace

1933 Westland-Houston PV-3

1933 Westland PV-7

1934 Parnell Hendy Heck

1934 Westland Pterodactyl V

1934 Westland F7/30

1934/35 Hawker Audax

1934/35 Hawker Hector

1936 Westland Lysander

1940 Westland Whirlwind

1941 Supermarine Spitfire

1942 Westland Welkin

1942 Fairey Barracuda

1943 Supermarine Seafire

1946 Westland Wyvern

1950's North American F86 Sabre

1954 JetLift Meteor

1960 Fairey Gannet

1934 Cierva C-29

1935 Cierva CL-20

1948 WS-51 Dragonfly

1958 WS-55 Whirlwind

1955 Westland Widgeon

1957 WS-58 Wessex

1958 Westland Westminster

1959 Bristol Sycamore

1959 Saunders Roe Skeeter

1959 Bristol Belvedere

1960 Fairey Rotodyne

1960 Westland Scout

1962 Westland Wasp

1965 Westland-Agusta/Bell 47G (Sioux)

1969 Sea King HAS

1973 Sea King Export

1977 Sea King HAR

1979 Sea King HC

1968 Aerospatiale Puma

1970 Gazelle

1972 Lynx AH Mk1/7

1972 Lynx HAS Mk2/3

1979 Westland 30

1982 Sea King AEW

1984 Super Lynx 300

1983 Lynx-3

1986 Westland W30 300

1987 WS-70 Black Hawk

1989 Merlin RN

1989 Lynx Mk9/9A

1989 Lynx Mk8

1996 Merlin RAF

1997 Merlin/Cormorant Export

2000 WAH-64 Apache

2013 AW159 Wildcat

2015 AW189

Appendix 2: Westland People

The founders of Westland, Percy and Ernest, twin brothers.

Left: Capt. Stuart Keep, first Chief Test Pilot, lost his legs in Dreadnought crash. Right: Robert Bruce, general manager, 1915–34.

Arthur Davenport, Harald Penrose and Robert Bruce, with the Everest aircraft, 1933.

Westland workers in a Vimy Bomber.

Harald Penrose, legendary Chief Test Pilot, 1931–53.

The Westland Home Guard Parade for the Duke of Kent, 1941.

W.E.W. Petter. Son of Ernest Petter, designer of Lysander, Whirlwind fighter, Welkin, Canberra and Gnat.

'Ted' Wheeldon played a prominent part in the policy change to build helicopters.

John Speechley. The first Westland Apprentice to become Managing Director.

O.L.L. Fitzwilliams led the design and development during the transition to helicopters.

The MacRobert Award recipients, 1975: David Balmford, Kieron MacKenzie, John Speechley, Vic Rogers and George Smith-Pert.

Pilots 1966: L. de-Vigne, P. Wilson, R. Crayton, J. Fay, K. Chadbourn, R. Gellatly, 'Slim' Sear, J. Morton, D. Farquehason, R. Moxam and D. Colvin.

Left to Right: Raoul Hafner, Rotorcraft Pioneer; Reggie Brie. Worked for Cierva and Westland. Led radar calibration flying using autogiros in the Second World War; Trevor Egginton, holder of the Absolute World Air Speed Record for helicopters, 1986.

First flight of EH-101 at Yeovil: Design, Development and Flight team, October 1987.

Appendix 3: Pictures of Westland

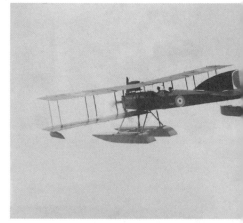

Clockwise from above left: The original 'Works Entrance' can still be found well inside the factory; The first aircraft built at Yeovil were Short 184 seaplanes; these were taken by rail to a coastal base for flight clearance. The de-Havilland DH.9A was built by Westland, and was the basis for the Wapiti and Wallace.

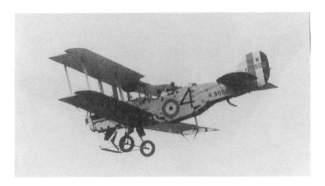

Walrus: Much of the activity after the First World War was based on the DH-9A, for which Westland held design authority.

The main girder structure for the Vimy hangar in 1919, which was the main office and flight shed until after the war.

The factory in 1947, the Westland railway siding both visible and active.

The Pterodactyl 4, one of the series of tailless designs tested 1925–35. This one even had hand-cranked variable geometry.

Lysander production beginning to ramp up for the war; the Lysander fared badly when up against the Luftwaffe. It was never intended for 'Blitzkrieg'.

Yeovil airfield, 1930. Note that the tone boundary is still well to the east of the airfield.

The Wapiti; over 500 were built and kept the firm active during the post-First World War depression.

Westland built two Autogyros for Cierva, 1934–35.

The prototype Westminster, intended to lead to a 40-seat civil and military helicopter.

The only occasion when the Westminster and the Rotodyne came together for Farnborough 1960. Flying from White Waltham.

Westland carried out the
modification and clearance of a
Meteor that was to lead to the
Harrier Jump Jet.

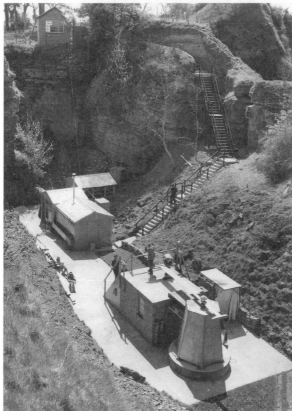

Ramjet experimental rig
installed on Ham Hill to
avoid noise in residential areas
(mid-1950s).

The Lynx ground running rig was installed at Yeovilton in 1969/70, testing transmission and the control system.

The Westland 30 was at the heart of the 'Westland affair'; the Series 300 incorporated BERP blades, five-bladed main and his tail rotor and improved airframe, but it was too late to make a difference.

The anti-submarine mission system some two years ahead of any opportunity to test it in the definitive aircraft.

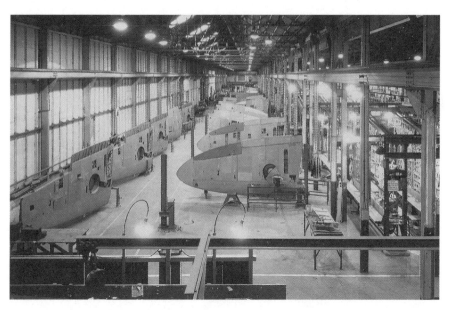

Spitfire and Seafire repair and production was maintained at Yeovil throughout the Second World War.

The awesome Apache carries missiles, rockets and a 37mm cannon, plus radar and video detection systems.

Bibliography

Fred Ballam

No book concerning Westland would be complete without reference to Fred Ballam, who joined Westland during the Second World War as an apprentice, was placed with Normalair during its founding years and returned to Westland where he quickly rose to Chief Instrumentation Engineer, a responsibility he held with distinction until he retired in 1988.

Fred was also a leading member of the Yeovil Branch of the Royal Aeronautical Society, a long-standing committee member, much of that as secretary. Perhaps one of Fred's great achievements was the establishment of a substantial archive of Westland records and artefacts, and part of that activity resulted in the following bibliography.

It is most appropriate that this should be associated with Fred's name, because a substantial number of the books included relied heavily on his help with information and photographs.

The comprehensive archive that has now been installed with management support is also a tribute to the difference motivated individuals can make.

The following bibliography was originally included in the AgustaWestland website. A few items have been added and in its present form it offers a useful reference, and includes many books that were published before the onset of ISBN numbers and so are recognised by date only.

It must be emphasised that it does not claim to be a complete record of all that has been published about Westland or the associated products.

Allen, P., *Sea King* (London: Airlife, 1993)

Allen, P., *Wessex* (London: Airlife, 1988)

Arkell, B., & Taylor, J., *Helicopters and VTOL Aircraft Work Like This* (London: J.M. Dent, 1972)

Andrews, C.F., & Morgan, E.B., *Supermarine Aircraft Since 1914* (London: Putnam, 1981)

Balance, T. & Sturtivant, R., *Squadrons of the Fleet Air Arm* (Tonbridge Wells: Air Britain, 1994)

Barnes, C.H., *Bristol Aircraft Since 1910* (London: Putnam, 1988)

Biasco, J.R., & Huertas, S.M., *Falklands – Witness of Battles* (Spain: Gremis, 1985)

Bingham, V., *Whirlwind* (Shrewsbury: Airlife, 1987)

Blacker, S., & Buchan, P.T., Douglas-Hamilton, D., Etherton, P.T., Fellowes, J., Stewart, L.V., *The 1933 Houston Mount Everest Expedition* (New York: Robert M. McBride, 1934)

Brown, E., *Wings of the Weird and Wonderful, Vol. 2* (Shrewsbury: Airlife, 1985)

Butler, T., *British Secret Projects* (Ian Allan)

Chartres, J., *Fly for their Lives* (Shrewsbury: Airlife, 1988)

Chartres, J., *The Westland Sea King: Modern Combat Aircraft 18* (Ian Allan, 1981)

Clark, F., *Agents by Moonlight* (Stroud: Tempus, 1995)

Davies, G., *From Lysander to Lightning: Teddy Petter* (Stroud: History Press, 2014)

Douglas-Hamilton, D., & McIntyre, D.F., *The Pilot's Book of Everest* (Edinburgh: William Hodge & Company, 1936)

Douglas-Hamilton, D., *Roof of the World: Man's First Flight Over Everest* (Edinburgh: Mainstream Publishing, 1983)

Dowling, J.R., *RAF Helicopters: The First Twenty Years* (London: HMSO, 1992)

Everett-Heath, J., *British Military Helicopters* (London: Putnam, 1974)

Fay, J., *The Helicopter: History, Piloting & How it Flies* (Newton Abbot: David & Charles, 1976)

Fiddler, *Fairey Gannet* (SOFFAAM)

Gibbings, D., *Fairey Rotodyne* (Stroud: History Press, 2009)

Gibbings, D., *Putting the Record Straight* (Picton, 1990)

Gibbings, D., *Sea King 1969–1990* (SOFFAAM)

Goulding, J., *Interceptor: RAF Single-Seat Multi-Gun Fighters* (London: Ian Allan, 1986)

Green, W., & Cross, R., *The Jet Aircraft of the World* (London: MacDonald, 1955)

Green, W., & Swanborough, G., *The Complete Book of Fighters* (London: Salamander, 1994)

Gunston, B., *Encyclopaedia of the World's Combat Aircraft* (Salamander)

Halley, J.J., *THE K FILE – The Royal Air Force of the 1930s* (Air Britain, 1996)

Halley, J.J., *Royal Air Force Aircraft AA100-AZ999* (Air Britain, 1985)

Halley, J.J., *Royal Air Force Aircraft DA100-DZ999* (Air Britain, 1987)

Halley, J.J., *Royal Air Force Aircraft EA100-EZ999* (Air Britain, 1988)

Halley, J.J., *Royal Air Force Aircraft P1000-R9999* (Air Britain, 1996)

Halley, J.J., *Royal Air Force Aircraft SA100-VZ999* (Air Britain, 1985)

Halley, J.J., *Royal Air Force Aircraft T1000-V9999* (Air Britain, 1989)

Halley, J.J., *Royal Air Force Aircraft V1000-W9999* (Air Britain, 1979)

Halley, J.J., *Royal Air Force Aircraft WA100-WZ999* (Air Britain, 1983)

Harrison, *Fairey Gannet AEW 3* (A.W. Hall)

Hawkins, M., *Somerset at War* (Wimbourne: Dovecote Press, 1988)

Hawkins, M., *Thanks for the Memory* (Somerset: Hawk Editions, 1996)

Jackson, A.J., *De Havilland Aircraft Since 1909* (London: Putnam, 1978)

James, D., *Dowty and the Flying Machine* (Stroud: Tempus, 1999)

James, D., *Westland (Images of England)* (Stroud: Tempus, 1997)

James, D., *Westland Aircraft Since 1915* (Putnam, 1991)

Lloyd, M., *The Guinness Book of Helicopter Facts and Feats* (Enfield: Guinness, 1993)

Lukins, A.H., *The Book of Westland Aircraft* (Harborough Publishing Co., 1943 & 1947)

Mason, F.K., *The British Fighter Since 1912* (London: Putnam, 1992)

Mason, F.K., & Hefferton, *British Flight Testing – Martlesham Heath* (Putnam)

Meekoms, K.J., & Morgan, B., *The British Aircraft Specifications File* (Air Britain, 1995)

Mensworth, E., *Family Engineers* (Ward Lock)

Mercer, N., *Fleet Air Arm* (Shropshire: Airlife, 1994)

Middleton, D.H., *Test Pilots – The Story of British Test Flying, 1903–1984* (Collins, 1985)

Milne, J.M., *Flashing Blades Over the Sea* (Maritime)

Monday, D., *Westland. Planemakers: 2* (London: Jane's, 1982)

Morgan, E.B. & Shacklady, E., *Spitfire: The History* (Key Pub Group, 2000)

Mottram, G., & Rippon, P.M., *Yeovilton: The History of the Royal Naval Air Station* (Fox & Co, 1990)

Nickel, K., & Wohlfahrt, M., *Tailless Aircraft in Theory and Practice* (Arnold/Hodder)

Oliver, D., *Battlefield Helicopters* (Osprey)

Ovcacik, M., & Susa, K., *Westland Lysander* (4+ Publications, 1999)

Ovcacik, M., & Susa, K., *Westland Wessex* (4+ Publications)

Penrose, H., *Adventure with Fate* (Shrewsbury: Airlife, 1984)

Penrose, H., *Airymous* (Airlife, 1982)

Penrose, H., *Cloud Cuckooland* (Shrewsbury: Airlife, 1981)

Penrose, H., *No Echo in the Sky* (London: Cassell, 1958)

Rawlings, J., & Sedgwick, H., *Learn to Test, Test to Learn: History of the ETPS* (Shrewsbury: Airlife, 1991)

Robertson, B., *Lysander Special* (London: Ian Allan, 1977)

Robertson, B., *The Westland Whirlwind* (Kookaburra, 1974 & 1980)

Robertson, F.A., & Colson, C.N., Cook, W.A., *Squadrons of the Royal Air Force* (Flight)

Sarkar, D., *Angriff Westland* (Worcester: Ramrod, 1994)

Schofield, Jim, *Developing British Military Helicopters* (Jim Schofield, 2010)

Sturtivant, R., *Fairey Aircraft* (Sutton, 1995)

Sturtivant, R., & Thompson, D., *Royal Air Force Aircraft J1-J999* (Air Britain)

Sturtivant, R., & Thompson, D., *Royal Air Force Aircraft K1000-K9999* (Air Britain, 1987)

Sturtivant, R., & Thompson, D., *Royal Air Force Aircraft K1000-K9999* (Air Britain)

Sturtivant, R., & Page, G., *Royal Navy Aircraft, Serials & Units* (Air Britain)

Tagg, A.E., & Wheeler, R.L., *From Sea to Air (Saunders-Roe)* (Isle of Wight: Crossprint, 1989)

Taylor, J.W.R., *Combat Aircraft of the World* (London: Ebury/Joseph, 1969)

Taylor, H.A., *Fairey Aircraft Since 1915* (Putnam, 1988)

Taylor, J.W.R., *Warplanes of the World* (London: Ian Allan, 1960)

Taylor, J.W.R., & Allward, M.F., *Westland 50* (London: Ian Allan, 1965)

Thetford, O., *Aircraft of the Fighting Powers Vol. 6* (Watford: Argus, 1980)

Thetford, O., *Aircraft of the Fighting Powers Vol. 7* (Watford: Argus, 1979)

Thetford, O., *British Naval Aircraft Since 1912* (Putnam)

Turner, J.F., *Hovering Angels* (London: Harrap, 1957)

Turner, J.F., *The Vickers Vimy* (Haynes)

Various, *75 Eventful Years – A Tribute to the Royal Air Force* (London: Lookturn, 1993)

Various, *A History of the Westland Wyvern* (Hampshire: BARG, 1973)

Verity, H., *We Landed by Moonlight* (Wilmslow: Air Data, 1995)

Welkin, & Meteor, *Camouflage & Markings – Whirlwind* (Decimus)

Wood, D., *Project Cancelled* (Tri-Service, 1990)

Profile Publications:

No 32 Wapiti (1958)

No 41 Supermarine Spitfire l & ll (1965)

No 159 Lysander (1960)

No 121 Sopwith 1½ Strutter (1960)

No 166 Supermarine Spitfire V Series (1967)

No 191 Whirlwind (1967)

Supermarine Seafire (Merlins) (1971)

No 248 de-Havilland DH-9A (1973)